Retirement Italiano:
Adventures and Misadventures in a Foreign Culture

TERRENCE COEN

ISBN: 978-1-7323736-1-7

Donaldson Bain Publishing
St. Petersburg, FL

DEDICATION

To Laura;
responsible for this adventure
and light of my life for more than half a century

From "Die slowly" by Martha Medeiros

"He who becomes the slave of habit,
who follows the same routines every day,
who never changes brand,
dies slowly.

Who does not risk certainty for uncertainty,
to thus follow a dream,
those who do not forego sound advice at least once in
their lives,
die slowly."

PROLOGUE

We reached Farnese in the mid-afternoon, hungry and a bit worn from the day's travels. Entering the *centro storico* (the historic old town) from the southeast, we passed under an arch and into a *piazza*. Except for a couple of parked cars that appeared to be of 1990s or older vintage, the *piazza* was empty. There were a few shops, but none showed any sign of life. We had heard that the population was, in polite terms, on the senior side. I wondered if they had all passed on.

Just when I was beginning to think that was the case, Laura spotted a real live human being, who was shuffling out of what turned out to be one of the town's two bars. I parked the car outside it, and we went in. We soon learned that neither of the bars served lunch and that—at that time of year—neither did the town's two restaurants. But, we were told, maybe if we hurried we could get a bite at the pizza parlor, although one never knew when it might be open or closed. Thankfully it was open that day.

We took a table in the empty dining room in the Pizzeria, and my thoughts went back to the time I first googled Farnese and learned it was a small town of some 1,600 inhabitants with—what I surmised—was an uncertain future. Now it struck me as a town stuck in time, or maybe even forgotten by time. Eventually we discovered that much of Farnese's appeal to us was a result of that time warp. It was more like the Italy that Laura had left so many years ago; more like the one I remembered from old black-

and-white Italian movies like *Cinema Paradiso* or *Yesterday, Today and Tomorrow*. It was truly Italian, so different from the Italy an average tourist views through the glass of a tour bus. It was the Italy we had so often daydreamed about.

As we walked through the town for the first time that spring day, I thought that we were encountering pretty hard looks or maybe just curious looks. Apparently, the locals were not too accustomed to welcoming visitors, except during the summer months, but in time we found out that once we struck a single friendship, we seemed to become friends with the entire town population.

THE GIG IS UP…TIME TO CALL IT A DAY

It hit me hardest on the day I found myself expounding upon the quality of our new Tupperware bowls to a friend. Was this the highlight of my day? I hadn't prepared for retirement. I needed a big dream and the chance to make it a reality. And surprisingly the opportunity hit me smack in the kisser.

This is my story of the rollercoaster ride of joys and challenges as I ended my corporate career and swapped my life in suburban Connecticut for a retirement (of sorts) in a small Italian village. A village located off the beaten path of tourism and pretty much stuck in an earlier time. It came about as my wife and I found ourselves managing a B&B, or what Italians call an *agriturismo*.

For nearly fifty years my life had been defined by my career as a marketer and my role as husband and father. With retirement on the horizon, my wife Laura and I looked forward to spending our days together. Admittedly each with some concern. For Laura it was sensing I was about to encroach on her territory. For me it was an undefined future. When a friend asked if I was prepared to "just live," I found myself stumbling to answer.

Our two daughters, Monica and Daniela, and son Francis had now been raised, educated and set free. They had successfully launched careers, married, bought homes and, in the case of Monica and Fran, procreated. No more graduations to attend, brides to give away, or sons to stand up for. Tuitions all paid. Counsel all provided whether needed or not. Responsible father role was now mischievous grandfather role.

As a business development guy, I built two companies from nearly scratch to positions of national and international market leadership. But as happens when shelf life dwindles down, the time eventually came to call it a day and depart Survey Sampling International, the Connecticut-based company that provides statistical samples to marketing researchers and opinion pollsters. Public opinion polls, concept tests, ad testing, harrowing deadlines, jet flights, board rooms, conference calls, budgets, forecasts, and alternatively inattentive and over-attentive equity investors occupied my days (and often my nights) as I helped to build a global leader. For the most part, I truly enjoyed those career years. A clipping on my desk quoting Goethe probably best sums it up: "A man can stand anything except a succession of ordinary days."

And happily and luckily the days had been extraordinarily good to me, so that when the time came for goodbyes, hugs, thanks and hastily scripted tributes from about to be former colleagues, chafing to get back to their offices, my asset management adviser assured me that, so long as I didn't make any rash investments, my Laura and I could take comfort in the fact that only due to some kind of divine intervention were we likely to see our days outlive our dollars.

At the leaving there was a cake and the presentation of an inscribed sterling silver golf tee from Tiffany's and assurances that I would be missed. For how long? I thought. Sixteen minutes was my best guess. A golf tee no less? Year in and year out, my identity had been entwined with the growth and success of the company. Any coworker who knew me at all was aware that, apart from my professional life, my passions were sailing and tennis. No way could I see myself filling empty days vainly trying to adjust my slice or hook and talking about birdies and bogeys. It was perfectly fine for my friends who had developed a passion for the game, but for me the small white ball and green hillside would be Sisyphus pushing the stone up the hill.

I quickly exchanged the well-intended but inappropriate gift for a silver heart-shaped necklace for Laura, a very small token for all the support she provided during those career years. Or maybe it was a little something to ease the trepidation of having to bear my intimidating transition to a state of life for which I felt totally unprepared. How many friends had said, "Terry, the best years of your life are your working years"?

In fact, I was in complete denial regarding my entry into this "golden state" called senior citizenship. My life had hit the wall. What would I do with myself? How would I fill my empty days with more than memories? I had been so engulfed in the thrills of the chase I never truly prepared for the finish line. I began to see my life as a movie on a

DVD. When the story concluded, all that remained was an innocuous collection of disconnected outtakes. Would we wrap it all up in Florida? God's waiting room surrounded by legions of overly tanned, prune-faced, waffle-cheeked contemporaries queuing up for the 4:30 key lime pie dinner special. *Would I begin the process of dying slowly?*

I tried to design a plan for what some did say would be the best years yet. Some decisions were easy. We would escape the cold Connecticut winters by spending time with our son, Fran, and his young family in sunny California. Some decisions were not so simple, like how to give back to the community. Some of my contemporaries told me about all the satisfaction they received from volunteering, and I did feel a certain need to give back. Yet a few meetings I "test attended" left me feeling that many golden agers, like small children, should be seen and not heard. I knew myself well enough to understand that ladling soup in a homeless shelter would not cut it. Having to take rather than give direction would not fit my comfort zone. I looked for other ways to get more involved in my community. But sadly, an attempt to serve on the local volunteer fire department proved rather futile.

Now I didn't have expectations of climbing ladders to rescue children from burning buildings, but I did think I could find a meaningful role. However, a couple of nights of standing in the cold while watching eighteen-year-olds learn to operate the jaws of death, coupled with a night racing through the streets of town in my fifteen-year-old Porsche in fast pursuit of the fire truck, convinced me that for the sake of my health, let alone the safety of the community at large, I would have to find another gig.

I had to find something more engaging or succumb to the truth that the new seventy wasn't the old forty like the media often proclaimed, but probably more like the old sixty nine. And then it happened.

It happened when Laura and I were attending The Waters Global Forum, a quasi-academic conference entitled, "The Art of War & Peace: Leadership & Human Nature." We were into some pretty heavy reading in preparation for the conference, and I derived much satisfaction from it, realizing that it was not the type of thing I would have had time for during my working days. The conference was in Rome, the city where my spouse of nearly half a century, the former Marialaura Ferrini, was born and had grown up.

Rather than stay in what we believed to be the overpriced hotel beneath the Spanish Steps (bulging with tourists) that served as the conference site, Laura made arrangements to rent a small apartment belonging to a friend of a woman she had met in Connecticut. The apartment was in a very nice neighborhood across the Tiber River and provided us with an opportunity to take a walk through the heart of Rome to the conference hotel. Each day for about 45 minutes, including a stop for cappuccino, we lived the lives of Roman pedestrians, testing different routes, while remaining on the alert for a constant onrush of cars and scooters (*motorini*) and other pedestrians. The crosswalks painted in horizontal stripes, referred to by the locals as "zebras," were supposed to afford protection, but it seemed we had to be looking in all directions at the same time. Drivers did seem pretty adept at either accelerating to rapidly pass in front or behind the pedestrians or brake at the very last minute. The *motorini* seemed especially menacing, as they were often hidden by *le macchine* (cars).

After the first morning I began to see the zebras as nonfunctioning demilitarized zones.

It puzzled me that Italians always drove in such a hurry when they seldom seemed to pay much heed to punctuality. It struck me that Italians have, at least by American standards, a peculiar relationship with cars and the laws that attempt to govern their use. I am not sure why this is. My best guess is that in the cities the number of cars exceeds the number of legitimate parking spaces. Finding a place to park in cities like Rome can lead to mounting frustration. I am often reminded of my Italian sister-in-law's indignation, when having driven to the local market, she discovered that some obviously inconsiderate motorist had the gall to park on the very same spot on the sidewalk that she considered, by some kind of unwritten law of previous usage, to be reserved for her alone.

Maybe once behind the wheel with the foot on the accelerator, the Italian driver experiences a sense of liberation from this type of bottled up frustration that causes him or her to throw caution to the wind. Or maybe it's nothing that specific, but rather a general need to feel unshackled from the overburdening, omnipresent bureaucracy that motivates them to ignore things like speed limits, seatbelt laws and one-way street signs. Behind the wheel in the car, they are in their own space.

I found our days in Rome very exhilarating and somehow a desire to become a deeper part of it all began to percolate inside me. After dinner in one of a variety of fine Roman restaurants following the conference discussions, Laura and I would enjoy an evening walk through the city marveling at illuminated ancient architecture. At the end of the walk, pleasantly exhausted in both mind and body, we would return to our apartment and a visit with our landlord. She was proving to be a cordial hostess and was extremely charming and kind toward us. One had to be impressed with her appearance and carriage. Tall in height with defined cheekbones, she had the mature good looks that signaled in her youth she must have been the type of Italian beauty seen in the Italian films of the 1960s and 70s. She gave us access to the rooftop terrace with a view across the city and the seven hills the ancient Romans built their city upon. We could not help but be impressed with her demeanor as she shared a bottle of wine with us while telling us about life as a painter and *professore* in Rome.

Then she told us of the *borgo*. Laura told me that a *borgo* was a small collection of buildings, much smaller than a village. The *borgo* in this case was a small collection of dwellings on the outskirts of the town of Farnese at the northern tip of the province of Lazio (the province of Rome). The region is agricultural and the *borgo* qualified as a *fattoria* or farm and further qualified as an *agriturismo*, which meant that it was licensed to host visitors, and as such, qualified for government assistance. "It lies about ten kilometers from the southernmost Tuscan border and about forty minutes to Umbria and the town of Orvieto going east," La Signora described in accented but clear English.

As the wine reached the bottom of the bottle, Laura began to thank our hostess and tell her how wonderful it was to be back in the land of her birth, signaling an end to the evening. But our hostess leaned forward, and in Italian confided that her own life in Italy had become somewhat burdensome, and she just wished she could find someone to take over the *borgo* for a while. Needing to translate the full conversation, Laura repeated in English: "La Signora said she and her husband had fallen out of love and split a dozen or so years back, and now managing the *borgo* and chasing back and forth to Rome feels anything but romantic."

I could tell just from the look on Laura's face that she was beginning to think that for the two of us, it truly could be romantic. La Signora went on to tell us that she had two grown sons and neither had any interest whatsoever in spending time at the *borgo*. As splendid as the property and associated lifestyle was for La Signora, it was nothing but an exhausting responsibility. If only she could put that responsibility aside for a while and just go to Iceland and paint. Iceland to paint? Of all places, I thought.

I guessed I had heard stranger things than leaving Italy for Iceland to go and paint, although I wasn't sure what. But what struck me most was not the unusual nature of her desire, but the potential opportunity for Laura and me to immerse ourselves in a new way of life. One that would satisfy the former Marialaura Ferrini's long-standing desire to live again for a time in Italy, and for us both an alternative to deck shuffleboard, reading e-mails about step-in bathtubs and bus tours from one Sun City or another. Could it be that we could start an exciting new chapter in our lives? After all, wasn't it a dream for many Americans to retire in Italy or open a B&B in their golden years? And here we were thinking of an opportunity to do both. I began to think that perhaps I was retiring from the information industry, but by no means was I retiring from life. Little did either of us know back then all that was in store for us.

BACK TO THE VERY BEGINNING

That night I had trouble falling asleep. I found myself thinking back nearly half a century ago. So often people would wonder how a ham and egger from New Jersey happened to be married to a lovely lady from Rome, Italy. When they would ask, I often took delight in fabricating tales describing our meeting. My favorite was to describe how my platoon had gallantly rescued her village during the "Big War." If I found them taking that in, I would proceed to embellish the story adding, "The lure of cigarettes, chocolate bars and nylon stockings was more than she could resist, and she followed us out of town."

Some listeners took it all in. Others would give a quizzical look, which would often lead to a tale somewhat more plausible for the time. "While we each happened to be visiting Venice, a big wind blew her hat across the piazza and into the Grand Canal. Undaunted, and although a non-swimmer, I dove in and rescued it. And we lived happily ever after." I gave that one up too when a friend took to adding that Laura also dove into the Canal, in order to rescue me.

The real story is very different. In truth, I drew a winning number in the lottery of life. Equipped with the first college degree in the family and my Marine Corps service behind me, I set out to find a career. My mom told me that the local high school was looking for a history teacher and didn't I have my degree in history?

And so there I was. My first day of school all over again. Back in the type of place I thought I had put behind me for good. But I had to begin a career and what other career was I suitably prepared for anyway?

The bell signaling the end of class rang, and as soon as the students left for their next class, I darted out into the hall, making a dash for the exit door and a few hasty puffs on a cigarette, my survival for feeling so out of my element.

Suddenly I was stopped in my tracks by the sight of a stunning young woman stepping out of a classroom down the hall, passively giving me a polite but disinterested nod and heading in the opposite direction.

Out in the courtyard, a fellow teacher informed me that I had just seen the new Spanish teacher. I remember thinking how lucky those high school Spanish students were to be able to gaze into her eyes for fifty minutes a day, five days a week. But how would they ever be able to concentrate on their grammar and vocabulary?

And of course at first I thought she was a Latina beauty. In time we got acquainted and I learned of her real Italian origins. Since my earliest adolescent years I had felt an attraction to young Italians of the fairer sex. I might have been all of twelve years old watching the Ed Sullivan Show when he introduced a teen opera singer from Pesaro, Italy, by the name of Anna Maria Alberghetti. I was knocked over by the television set. Mesmerized by her beauty, I felt a new sensation as it dawned on me that Italy produced more than popes, cardinals and pizza pies. I was convinced she would like to step out from the television set and take my hand. Become my special friend. Puppy love.

The bar was set very high from that moment. And now about ten years later, I was beginning to experience the same sensations. Oh those eyes. She was the real thing. Marialaura Ferrini from Rome by way of Barry College in Miami, Florida. As we got acquainted I learned how she came to be teaching at the school. That she came to the states at the invitation of an uncle to spend a semester at the college in order to learn English. And how the six months turned into three years and a degree with highest honors, which led to a desire to test life in America outside the college environment.

Awkwardly I courted her. First over a glass of cider, which she declined, when we chaperoned the school Halloween dance. Then an invitation to a local New Year's Eve Party, which she did accept. More interested in each other than sharing in the New Year's reverie, we left the party a bit early. I was smitten and the courtship took on the resemblance of a full court press. When the school closed for spring break we drove to Fort Lauderdale to meet her aunt and uncle. When the school year ended Laura returned to Rome where her parents, who had never ventured outside of Rome and its environs reluctantly accepted the fact that their youngest daughter had fallen in love with an American. Back in New Jersey, I would fret that they would succeed in persuading her to abandon such a foolish idea and remain in Rome. The mail from Italy was tortoise slow and I agonized as weeks went by without any word and the three letters written weeks ago would arrive on the same day.

In the fall Laura returned as planned and I began a business career in magazine advertising in New York City, determined to earn enough money to support a marriage and what might come with it. At Christmas we became engaged and in August with her mother having made the trip from Italy, we married.

Hard to believe that so many years had gone by since that time. Strange how things happen. Boy, did luck ever come my way!

And so we developed in our careers. I enjoyed a business career, and Laura eventually became a garden designer. Along the way we raised three children, saw them married off to extremely suitable partners, wound down our careers, and then (with me in heavy denial) qualified for Medicare and began to receive discounts at ski resorts and movie houses.

And now just perhaps the good fortune might continue with a new chapter in the Italian countryside.

Or perhaps not.

OUR FIRST VISIT TO THE BORGO

The conference had ended and Laura and I found ourselves riding with our landlord, now new friend and potential partner, to Farnese to view the *borgo*, complete with a seven-bedroom main house. Laura explained that the main residence was known as the *casale*, and the four adjoining apartments were created from one of the stone barns. We anticipated viewing the twenty-some acre fields complete with 252 century-old olive trees in the grove just behind the small vineyard.

We peppered La Signora with questions. "How far from Lake Bolsena was it? How long would it take to drive to the sea? How many ancient Etruscan ruins?" Our imaginations took over. Etruscan ruins and garden tours, bringing artists from the states to capture the countryside on their canvasses. Inviting friends over to share pasta and *vino locale*. And bringing the six grandkids over to learn why their grandmother is called "Nonna."

The journey seemed to be taking forever. I checked my watch and well over a half hour had gone by and we were not even outside of Rome. At times we inched forward. Then we would make a turn onto an open road and La

Signora would gun it as if impatient to reach the next bottleneck, reduced to another crawl. Eventually we reached the A1A and began to proceed at a semi-normal pace from town to town, heading north and west across the region of Lazio. I wasn't sure which I admired more, the ancient towns and small cities or the beautiful green and gold countryside with an occasional stone or stucco farmhouse, complete with red-tiled roofs and partly surrounded by rows of Italian cypress trees stretching toward the sky or scattered, umbrella-shaped pines. The landscape reminded me of Laura's favorite symphony, Respighi's "Pines of Rome." It is a beautiful piece in its own right and now whenever I hear it with Laura, I recall the Appian Way bordered by columns of the beautiful trees.

The towns and villages impressed me as living collages of the ancient and the modern. Signage advertising the fruits of twenty-first century technology was superimposed on ancient buildings along narrow roads, the fruits of the Roman Empire or Medieval fiefdoms. Some seem to be an okay fit, while others simply interrupted what I considered historical integrity.

Approximately an hour and a half from the time we began our journey, we exited onto an unpaved road and wound our way up a series of sharp turns until we approached an especially long concrete and stone building, set back just a few feet from the road. Laura's face reflected disappointment as La Signora parked the car and opened the metal gate to an archway that provided entry to the back acreage. Her expression changed as we proceeded through the arch and took in the gardens, patios, outbuildings, fields, and distant vineyard and olive grove. It seemed that the sight was radiating with character, but missing a healthy dose of tender loving care.

After parking the car, La Signora motioned us to what appeared to be the main entrance, where she proceeded to fetch a string of keys from her purse and to address a series of door locks. She opened the door, muttering in Italian something that I did not understand, but guessed referenced security and satisfaction. As we stepped inside the house a grey cat ran past us and bolted out the door. Strange, but dismissed by the thought of stepping back into history.

La Signora led the tour. The *casale*, or main house, contained seven bedrooms, as well as four apartments each containing a single bedroom. The *casale* had a large formal dining room, an adequate kitchen and a formal parlor. All were connected by long hallways containing paintings by La Signora, interspersed with other pieces of art. Each turn in the hallway and each landing on the stairs included a marble statue perched atop a pedestal.

The apartments contained vaulted or barrel-shaped ceilings, reflecting their earlier existence as places for storing the harvest and housing the animals. The barred windows from the upstairs bedrooms and second floor apartment opened to views of the surrounding fields and more distant hillsides.

There were still a number of rooms that had not been converted and stood exactly as they must have a century ago or more. One contained a large wooden barrel, probably a dozen feet in diameter and a massive wine press

to go with it. All manner of farming implements lay
scattered about.

La Signora prepared a lunch in the well-equipped but
incredibly cluttered kitchen while expounding upon how
visitors could not get enough of the *borgo*. Next we were
treated to a drive around the countryside. First the lake and
then a number of the charming villages that lay along the
Tuscany border. La Signora provided an endless narration
as Laura and I sat speechless, struggling to digest the
remarkable beauty.

Back in Rome we hurried through a light supper and went
to bed with no intentions of immediately falling to sleep.
Laura and I discussed what we loved about the place and
what needed to be improved. I loved its classical appeal,
and thought it only needed a little TLC. Laura pictured how
the dull earth-colored façade would come to life with some
simple window boxes and potted plants on the front
staircase. She wondered if this might indicate the *borgo* was
available to the locals for their visitors. I didn't imagine it
would take significant sums to take over the running of the
borgo. Not the least bit sleepy, I could feel the wheels
turning as I considered doing a deal, a very small but very
glamorous deal.

And so we began to create our business plan. The *borgo* and
surrounding Farnese were ideally suited for artists to ply
their crafts. The grain barn had already been converted into
a studio. It was spacious and bright, and the old chestnut
beams lent a charm that we just knew would add to the
artists' inspiration.

The place would have plenty of room, accommodating up to twenty visitors. The backfields would be mowed, creating a meadow for strolling in the evening and space for children to romp about or kick a soccer ball. Canvas umbrellas could be patched and set up over the patios to accommodate al fresco dining.

We began to list potential art teachers and draft a plan to provide free room and board to any instructor who could fill most of the *borgo's* bedrooms. It was a simple proposition. The instructor puts a program together, recruits his or her students for that program, and is compensated from the fees. We get the revenue from the rooms and the meals. We would be in the hospitality business, and with just a modicum of success we could cover the costs of living in Italy for a reasonable spell.

FROM DREAM TO REALITY

Back home in Connecticut we followed up with our potential landlord. What if we agreed to make La Signora all of her prior year's revenue, less expenses, and then share equally any additional profits we might create by promoting the property in the American market?

La Signora agreed with the proposition and advised us by e-mail that last year the property produced a net income of 50,000 euros. We responded that such an amount was way beyond anything we had imagined, and that we were sorry but no Italy for us and no Iceland for La Signora.

The next morning we awoke to see another e-mail apologizing for inadvertently having added an extra zero. We wanted to consider it an honest mistake, but I somewhat suspected that it was an Italian form of negotiation. In time I would learn that in Italy, much of life is a negotiation and very little is upfront.

So, for 5,000 euros we had our deal, and now it was time to work our plan. In addition to reaching out to the local artists, we decided to test viral marketing and engage our daughter Daniela to create a website.

I AM WORKING AGAIN

The networking began. Lunch with local Artist and friend Tom Ranges and his artist friend led to another lunch and another artist. Inquiries came in from around the web. We were happily engaged in the process, but time went by with no sales.

I began to have second thoughts. But we persisted and began to diversify. We added an offer for chefs, who could offer Italian cooking classes. After doing some significant research, Laura put together a list of gardens in the regions, eventually publishing brochures promoting the Secret Gardens of Italy. A friend who publishes a gardening newsletter introduced us to a woman who had developed a database of Master Gardeners and opened a garden touring business. She was ecstatic about putting together a group to tour Italian gardens while staying at the *borgo*. Now we were firing away! Going on all cylinders!

But still no one had signed on. That is, no one except for our children and grandchildren. What could be better than the thought that they would be joining us for a part of the summer, even though their visits would go into the expense rather than revenue column.

Weeks went by and no artists, chefs or gardeners signed on. We were not discouraged, although my pride was beginning to show a few bruises. What kind of a marketer had I turned out to be anyway? How could I be failing to sell this little piece of paradise?

It seemed that where existing programs were concerned, locations had been established long in advance. And artists and cooks were not content to just go to Italy; they wanted to go to Tuscany! It struck me that there was a misconception among many Americans that the Italian sun only shines in Tuscany.

Then finally, we had a bit of a breakthrough. I ran into Dmitri Wright, an artist acquaintance, who has a strong reputation as an impressionist painter and teacher. When I asked a mutual friend if Dmitri might be interested in Italy, he told me that, although Dmitri actively taught and had a strong following, his style would not lend itself to a program in Italy. So you can imagine my happy surprise when Dmitri's eyes began to light up as I described the *borgo*, Farnese and all that we had in mind. He shook his head in disbelief. What we were planning to do was just what he was looking to find.

So Dmitri and his wife, Karen, joined Laura and me for dinner, and over a second glass of wine, we began to roll out what each of us would need to do to put a program in August together. We really liked the Wrights, and the thought of them sharing a part of the summer with us was very pleasing. Karen, being an organizer par excellence, was properly cautious, so we decided that she and Dmitri could come to the *borgo* as our guests prior to the program to be sure that all would be ready. That way they could get the lay of the land.

We had our first instructor booked, and I entered Dmitri Wright's Plein Air Workshop on the calendar. All Dmitri and Karen needed to do was recruit the students. And I felt that given his reputation and Karen's dedication to the project, we could be reasonably certain that our first program would become a reality.

However, we needed to find more Dmitris, and while I had correspondence with art instructors from as far away as Tel Aviv, we continued to face the challenges that plans had been made and locations selected years ahead, or that any place in Italy would be great so long as it was in Tuscany. And then I happened upon our next instructor/partner. It happened on an unseasonably warm March day when my friend Bob Dowling and I set out to inaugurate the cycling season. While pedaling through town and approaching the Rowayton Art Center, I noticed a sign indicating that Will McCarthy was conducting a workshop. I hadn't met Will, but a work in oil depicting his impression of the Tuscan landscape hung in our living room. Laura and I both considered it our favorite piece of art. Why hadn't I contacted Will? No time like the present. I told Bob I needed to take five, hopped off the bike, and entered the art center, interrupting the workshop. Surrounded by the puzzled faces of students, who no doubt wondered what this old guy in the biking outfit was doing, I interrupted the class they had paid good money to attend.

I approached Will and blurted out, "I am seeking an art instructor for a program in Italy this coming summer." He gave me a blank look that soon changed into a "you have got to be kidding" look, and ended up with an intrigued look, responding that he just might be our next man. We agreed to follow up so as not to further interrupt his class. I rejoined Bob and my bicycle, hopeful but at the same time concerned that, once Will learned he would need to recruit the students himself, our budding relationship would become history.

I later learned that as soon as I left the art center, Will turned to the class and announced, "That guy just asked me to teach a workshop in Italy. Would any of you be interested in attending?" Three students said they would. And in September the three of them and other students of Will did attend.

A TEST RUN

After the meeting with Will, we began to feel that we had at least the nucleus of a business, and with a small feeling of relief decided to head off to Farnese for both making arrangements and doing a reality check.

In all candor, as the departure date grew nearer I had to confess to some creeping reservations about giving up a summer in our waterside home on Bell Island, in Connecticut, to spend part of the year in a foreign land. After all, apart from a brief stint in the Marine Corps, I had lived my entire life within a fifty-mile radius of New York City, which I always considered to be "the center of the universe." Sure I had traveled a fair portion of the globe in pursuit of business, but I always returned home after a few days, a week or two at most. Human nature being what it is, I began to fear that our plans might be falling apart. But I was thirsty for the adventure and most of all warmed by Laura's enthusiasm for what we sensed was lying ahead. We were not going to be ones to "Die Slowly."

Shortly after we arrived in Italy, those reservations were reinforced. The rental car agency did not have the *Cinquecento* (Fiat 500) we had reserved, and after more than an hour, when we did finally succeed in obtaining a car, it took four or five laps around Leonardo Da Vinci Airport before we succeeded in finding the exit. The GPS insisted on misdirecting us in Italian. I was tired from the flight over and a little frustrated with having to tolerate a somewhat dictatorial female voice coming from the machine. It was the poor pronunciation of her native language that got to Laura as she fumbled to try and change the language to English, while simultaneously translating for me.

"*Sinistra*," spoke the machine.

"Left," said Laura.

"I know," I replied. After all I had learned some Italian.

"Not that left. The other left."

As I started to make a U turn, the machine spoke out once more in what I interpreted as a reprimand.

"*Stupido*," Laura sighed.

"Huh?" I grumped.

"Not you."

To my relief, Laura directed her annoyance at the voice on the defenseless instrument and not at this hapless driver. She did so in two languages at that! The directions were hopelessly out of date, and I started to feel an uneasy sense of dependency, taking directions from not one but two women.

I shook it off, refocusing my attention on a fat black Mercedes bearing down on us with headlights flashing. "Italian drivers are not patient," I grumbled. That is an understatement. Life in Italy would not be without challenges. Another understatement, I would soon learn.

But it wasn't too long before we had safely arrived at Laura's sister Adriana's house and were sitting down to lunch of a peppery hot *brodo*, or soup, followed by stewed rabbit which she had marinated overnight to bring out every morsel of rich flavor. Of course, this was accompanied by a bottle of *vino locale*.

As the meal progressed to fruit and a variety of fresh cheeses, I couldn't help but consider a photo on the wall showing Adriana smiling at her late husband Goffredo, gone nearly ten years. My thoughts drifted to an advertisement for British Airways I frequently saw in tube stations while chasing down business in London during my former life. It depicted a forlorn-looking elderly couple sitting across the table from one another staring off rather blankly. It bore the headline: "I wish we had taken that trip to New York back then." The picture told me they had chosen to "Die Slowly." That was not for me. I did not want that to be us looking back sadly, wishing we hadn't followed through and started a new life managing an *agriturismo* in Farnese. After all we were just passing through this life and I wanted to make the most of it.

I remembered the advice from a good-hearted but not overly ambitious boss: "T, this ain't the dress rehearsal." That was over forty years ago but often seemed like just a few weeks ago. I kicked back from Adriana's table beginning again to feel the surge of initial excitement I had experienced when we first considered our Italian venture late last year.

The next morning, we rose early, bid Adriana a *grazie* and a *ciao* and headed north on Via Cristoforo Colombo to reconnect with Farnese and the *borgo*. Farnese was still in the midst of awaking from an unusual winter that actually had brought a few snowfalls. And so, that was the day we entered the empty pizza parlor, the only establishment open in town. This would be our real introduction to life in Farnese.

We entered and exchanged greetings with Valentina Di Blasio, the woman behind the counter. She directed us to sit anywhere in the empty dining room. We took a table and began to study the menu. Despite my limited command of the Italian language, I do okay with restaurant menus. Italian meals can serve as remarkable motivators.

From Valentina, who with her husband, Giancarlo, owned and ran the pizza parlor, we learned that the economy was primarily agricultural and that the local farmers still proudly employed the same techniques as their parents and grandparents.

"So how can they compete in world markets?" Laura asked. Valentina shrugged. Farnese was by no means ready for globalization. Valentina told us that the town boasted two *frantoi* or olive-oil cooperatives, a cheese factory, a bank, a post office, an occasionally open barber shop, and the local hardware store that we cynically referred to as "The Home Depot." The hardware store seemed to typify the difference between Farnese and our lives back in Connecticut. Aisles were small and cluttered and inventories sparse. We later joked that one trip to the hardware store would usually corner the entire market for any given item that we might have had the good fortune to find in the first place.

There are three small grocery stores in Farnese and three *forni* (bakeries) that provide the residents with their daily bread. Numerous hairdressers ensure that the ladies of Farnese keep up appearances. They usually work out of their homes, hidden from the *Guardia di Finanze*, whose job it is to collect taxes. The town also has four churches and three chapels.

One of Farnese's small claims to fame is that scenes from the 1972 TV miniseries *Le Avventure di Pinocchio* were filmed there. Valentina said residents still take pride in the fact that their town was selected for the filming and that many of its citizens filled in as extras.

Laura and I discussed what she recalled from her school days and what I'd learned from my web work. The Farnese name has historical significance, for the Farnese family was a powerful force during the Middle Ages. A powerful Farnese duke ruled over much of Tuscia, and Pope Paul III, a Farnese, served as pontiff in the sixteenth century when the papacy was both a temporal and secular power.

Today, *Il Palazzo Farnese* in Caprarola, on the other side of the provincial capital, Viterbo, is a magnificent, well-preserved palace, complete with spectacular gardens. In Rome the *Piazza Farnese* is a popular meeting place. But today the small town bearing the Farnese name is pretty much forgotten, although a few savvy Romans are beginning to snap up townhouses at bargain prices and renovate the interiors.

The arches that give access to the *centro storico* support an ancient walkway. According to local lore, the Duke of Farnese and his family used it to get about the town without having to encounter their unwashed subjects. The walkway now belongs to a lovely young woman named Rosaria, who uses it as a studio for gilding and a gallery where she displays some truly magnificent creations. Her hope is to someday restore the entire arch in a manner that will make it inviting to tourists. Most of the old town itself sits on a rock, and many of the homes overlook the vast national forest known as the Lamone.

The streets of the *centro storico* are cobbled and meander about in no particular pattern that I could discern. Each turn through its maze presents a new visual delight: brightly painted doors or window boxes spilling over with flowers, which contrast the background of muted stonework beautifully.

We enjoyed an amazingly inexpensive lunch of pasta with *porcini* (mushroom) and *gamberi* (shrimp), followed by a heaping plate of wild boar and a bottle of *vino locale*. It seemed to make sense to order a bottle so we could enjoy a glass or so at lunch and bring the remainder back to the *casale* to have with dinner, but somehow when the lunch was finished, so was the bottle. As we enjoyed the remaining sips, the restaurant owner, Giancarlo, proudly showed us the photo of his hunting team and the eighteen *cinghiali* (wild boars) they had bagged this past November.

THE MEMORABLE NIGHT AT THE BORGO

Soon after we arrived in town we met the Polish couple, Josef and Maria, who cared for the *borgo* property. Communications were difficult particularly with Josef, who managed to let us know that he spoke neither English nor Italian but perfect Polish. Just another challenge. We would manage. With Maria we checked out the *casale*, all seven bedrooms and all six bathrooms, noting that La Signora had left all the beds made up and the bedrooms looking very neat and clean, a contrast to the state of the rest of the property. We then successfully flushed all toilets and ran all sinks and showers. We did the same in all three apartments and then set about exploring the barns that were to serve as studios for the art class and the *forno* (bakery) where we hoped to roast sausage and make pizza. We measured and photographed the stoves, still hoping to do some cooking classes.

Everything checked out, so we made our way to the rooftop terrace to soak in the pastoral views. The sky was too hazy for us to see the Mediterranean Sea, but the hills and fields sparkled in the setting sun. The rooftop afforded a view of the cemetery. And like cemeteries throughout Italy, it was a work of art with clustered monuments and mausoleums and no shortage of fresh flowers.

With the beautiful scene surrounding us, neither of us had any reservations about trading our view of Long Island Sound, the Norwalk Islands and the NYC skyline for a season in this bucolic setting. After a while, I found myself literally counting sheep in the distant fields, so we determined it was time to light up the fireplace and prepare a bit of supper.

Soon we discovered that in spite of the roaring fire, there was no way to offset the evening chill. I turned to Laura and declared, "Perhaps we should spend this first night at a local hotel. These walls are thicker than my head and they refused to surrender to winter. They are sucking every ounce of warmth out of me."

Laura shook her head and responded, "You are in Farnese. There are no hotels." After a couple rounds of wandering around, locating portable heaters, blowing circuit breakers and fumbling in the dark, we finally were able to slide under half a dozen layers of blankets and doze off, concerned about how we would manage to get hot water in the morning.

"If there is any consolation," Laura said, "it is the thought that the wide stone walls will most likely maintain their Antarctic temperatures and air condition the building well into July and August."

CHECKING OUT THE TOWN

We began the next morning with a fifteen-minute stroll down the road past the cemetery, the olive oil *frantoio* (a processing plant where the juice is squeezed from the fruit and bottled), the school where they filmed the Pinocchio movie, and into the town. Cappuccinos, *cornetti* (croissants) and a Chamber of Commerce type pep talk from an enthusiastic barista came next. She gave lots of good advice about renting boats on the lake, finding the Capodimonte Tennis Club, and what to expect in general. It seemed like we were in store for an absolutely fabulous summer.

It was nearly noon when La Signora roared up in her SUV, dressed to the nines in a tweed suit, looking every bit the Roman patrician, successful artist and *professore*. Soon she was showing Laura the nuances of the main kitchen and preparing a *pranzo* (lunch) of *pasta al pesto* (spaghetti with a sauce of basil, olive oil, garlic and pine nuts). Lunch was followed by regaling accounts of how her family acquired and restored the property, which had served as a headquarters for Garibaldi during the war to liberate Italy from papal control. She described how the Germans took it from the family during World War II to serve as a command post. A somber tone emerged as she sadly recounted how two American soldiers were captured and imprisoned in the *cantina* and then murdered as the Nazi command fled the oncoming American army.

After lunch, we decided to take the short drive over the Tuscan border to Pitigliano and Sorano to check out the wine co-op and thermal spa. We happily noted that in addition to the thermal baths, the spa contained a large swimming pool that our grandchildren and children of guests might enjoy. I more happily noted that the wine co-op appeared to contain enough godly nectar to fill all the spas and pools many times over, and at ungodly low prices! All one needed to do was to bring their jugs to the *cantina*, where the attendant would fill them from a metered pump similar in appearance to gas pumps back home.

Back at the *borgo* we met with Rosaria, who maintains a studio in town to gild and restore antiques. She also teaches the art of gilding. We talked about how she might attract visitors from the states and the UK to stay at the villa and learn the craft of a true artisan.

Next came a meeting with Amabile, who was auditioning to cook for our guests on those evenings when they chose to eat in rather than enjoy a local *ristorante*. Amabile translates to "lovable," and she lives up to her name. In time we also met her husband, Reno, who has the hearty good looks of an Italian matinee idol and the deep baritone voice of an opera star. Amabile, whose day job was running the local bakery, passed the test with flying colors.

Laura and I were beginning to feel more comfortable with our landlord/partner. I had especially experienced some concerns when La Signora's e-mail quoting last year's revenue contained an extra zero which she subsequently proclaimed to be a typing error.

The rest of the week seemed to play out in the blink of an eye. We drove twenty minutes to the fish market in Marta, one of five towns scattered along the shores of Lake Bolsena, where one can purchase fresh perch, *corregone*, eel, and other tasty delights from the lake. Alternatively, the market offers whatever tasty bounty the Mediterranean Sea, just a half hour away, provided.

Next we discovered an attractive beach club on the lake, just twenty minutes from the *borgo*, called Paradise Beach. Before going to the beach we took lunch at the restaurant next door, appropriately named Il Purgatorio.

"This makes sense," I told Laura. "Before going to paradise Catholic doctrine and Dante have most people going to purgatory." As we enjoyed the local fish and *vino*, Laura responded, "If this is purgatory, I can't help but wonder what Paradise could possibly be like."

"And if anyone does not feel ready for these fine places, there is a church conveniently located just across the street where one can pray for forgiveness or offer a penance," was all I could think to say.

We travelled to Viterbo, the largest city and seat of the province and made arrangements with three new friends, Sergio, Stefano and Simone of the Try Nature agency, to line up some archeological and garden tours for the visitors who would be coming to the *borgo*. We then headed back to Rome for dinner with Adriana, a night's sleep, and a return flight to Connecticut the next day. We left feeling delighted that things were fitting into place. Just a bit concerned about our landlord/partner.

BACK HOME AND THINGS STARTED TO FALL IN PLACE

We had received an e-mail from Dmitri that his first students had registered for the sketching class he would be conducting in August. We also looked forward to a Friday meeting with Katie Melvin, who had just started a Garden Touring business and who hoped to lead groups to the Secret Gardens arranged by Laura in late June and early September. Will McCarthy checked in. He was definitely on board and had begun to publicize a workshop entitled "Painting From Memory and Imagination," which we scheduled for early September.

So, a few weeks later, having rented our Connecticut house and brimming with happy expectations, we repacked our bags and headed off to live in Italy for a season.

JUST A SLIGHT HICCUP

Before we knew it, we were less than twenty four hours out of JFK, sitting in a charming harborside restaurant, enjoying fresh seafood washed down by a pint of a dark liquid with a white top. A Guinness, no less. Twas all delightful, but we were a wee bit off plan. For the sea was not the Mediterranean, not Lake Bolsena, but sure and be glory twas the Irish Sea. The connecting flight from Dublin to Rome left without passengers in seats 13A and 13B. Namely us.

As we attempted to clear customs on our connecting flight from Dublin to Rome, I managed the two carry-ons and Laura her purse and our two tennis rackets. Early in my business life I experienced a number of trips where my checked luggage and I ended up going in different directions, so we developed the habit of carrying on.

I have been known to boast about the business trip where I circled the globe with just a carry-on and briefcase. And I delighted in telling about the traveler who approached the airline counter and requested, "I would like a ticket to Paris and to have my suitcases sent to Anchorage, Rio, Budapest and Johannesburg."

To which the airline attendant responded, "That would be impossible, sir."

"Why?" the traveler responded. "You did that the last time."

Sadly, our situation turned out to be just as amusing. As we approached the scanner to pass through security, a belligerent security guard bellowed something along the lines of, "You, lass, need to check those tennis rackets."

All within earshot halted and looked around as he repeated his command even louder. He was visibly annoyed, and I wondered if he was going to assault Laura. Startled, I had visions of her being dragged off to an interrogation room, pistol-whipped and cajoled to confess her membership in the Irish Republican Army, leaving me wandering about the Dublin airport trying to find where they had taken her. Irish airport security was on steroids. Weapons of terror? If only they knew how inaccurate I am when on the court with a tennis racket.

As a result of our security predicament, we missed our flight and spent the next two hours trying to persuade Fergus O'Malley and Sinead McMurphy and the rest of the authorities at Aer Lingus that they were responsible for the completion of our trip to Rome.

"Sorry, but it is your responsibility to abide by the rules, and besides there is only one seat to Rome available until Friday, at full fare to boot," reprimanded one of the security officers. Such a way to be treated in the land of my ancestors! Eventually we prevailed and enjoyed a bonus day in Ireland compliments of Aer Lingus. And then the next morning we went on to our extended stay in Italy.

LAURA FACES THE CARABINIERI

While the misadventure in Ireland turned out quite well, after having picked up our rental car and having spent the night at Adriana's in Rome, we found ourselves in an actual interrogation room. Sometime the previous night a vengeful Italian decided to redecorate my newly acquired French license-plated Peugeot. He or she had keyed several "racing stripes" on one side. I was beyond livid and bent on obtaining justice. To further complicate matters, Laura's credit card was missing and had to be reported. After waiting an inordinate amount of time in the anteroom, we laid our situation out in front of a very young, very bored officer of the Carabinieri, the Italian national police. They are the ones who always dress in red, white and blue uniforms, which I feel resemble parade attire. The Carabinieri is actually one of Italy's four military units, with origins in the Kingdom of Sardinia prior to the unification of Italy.

As we started our tales of woe, the young man was interrupted by a phone call. It went on and on. With my limited understanding of the Italian language, I had no notion of what he was dealing with. From time to time he rolled his eyes, took the phone from his ear and gestured toward us. Laura understood and had quite a laugh. She explained to me that the caller was complaining of a neighbor's dog that had been barking for three days. The young officer responded disdainfully that his job is to arrest people, not dogs. Exasperated, he turned to us and exclaimed that he wished he was an American cop, who according to the movies he had seen, solves all problems by simply shooting people.

And so we registered our complaint. Myriad forms were filled out and vigorously stamped many times over. I wondered if the simple solution to reforming Italy's overwhelming, overbearing bureaucracy would be to simply take away all the stamps. We left after receiving assurances by the officer that our complaints had been duly registered, and we could be assured that absolutely nothing would come of it.

SETTLING INTO LIFE IN FARNESE

Our first full week in Farnese we focused on settling in. For one thing, we selected our bar, a place called Rokkabar. There are two bars in Farnese, so a choice had to be made, but the staff at Rokkabar made this an easy decision. Two young and rather diminutive sisters own it and clearly got so much joy from their enterprise that it spilled out to all who patronized it. Laura and I often liked to start the day with a walk into town, under the arch and up the hill to Rokkabar, where we were greeted with *"Due cappuccini fuori?"* (two cappuccinos outside). We then wandered out to a table in the back, where shortly two cappuccinos were delivered. No need to rush. Time to observe and eventually strike up acquaintances. Italians usually take their coffee or alternative morning beverage standing at the bar, jabbering with the barista and other customers until their drink is served (often with a flourish on the part of the barista), quickly downing it and then going about their day. The exception to this are those times when they are meeting with friends. On those occasions they will sit together at a table and engage with one another and often folks at adjoining tables for extended amounts of time.

It was at a time like this that we struck up an acquaintance which led to a rich friendship and insights into our adopted Italian home. That day, just two tables away, sat two families whose conversation caught my attention. I realized that rather than hearing the musical but indiscernible Italian language, they were speaking English, or at least a form of it. When I made our presence and my mother tongue known to them, I learned that I was hearing Italian spoken with an accented Irish brogue. Liam O'Brien introduced his family and friends. The latter were his relatives visiting from Ireland, while his wife was a native Farnesean, who had migrated to Dublin where they found the romance that eventually produced their three attractive, bilingual offspring.

We chatted with the O'Briens for quite a while promising to visit one another soon. Then we turned our attention to the bustling *piazza*. It was a Thursday and Thursdays are a special day as the entire *piazza* turns into a sort of shopping mall. Sometime between 10:30 the night before, when we left dinner and town, and nine in the morning, the caravans entered town and set up shops displaying their wares, which ran from working pellet stoves to roasting *porchetta*, a delicious pork dish. It struck me that there was enough apparel on display to clothe all of Italy. And if you took all of the English words emblazoned on the shirts and jackets, you would have a vocabulary the size of the average seventh grader; however, with logos like "Power Off" and "Long Board Simpson," you would not be able to say anything that made the slightest bit of sense.

Pricing for most goods was a matter of negotiation. I saw a pair of jeans that I could use and inquired as to the cost, understanding that whatever the vendor quoted would simply be the first shot in a negotiation. I was prepared for the special high price I would get as an obvious visitor. We played it out, and with a keen sense of satisfaction I was in the process of declaring myself the victor and plunking down ten euros for the jeans when Laura intervened. The look she shot me said, "Back off," as she proceeded to run her fingers across the fabric while shaking her head back and forth. A protracted dialogue between Laura and the smiling vendor followed and concluded with the final price. Ten euros. She shook her head again and walked away. I thought it all a part of the game, expecting the vendor to call after her. But he did not. And I didn't get the jeans.

"But honey," I said. "What happened? I could use them, and I managed to get him down to ten."

"That can't be his best price. He is jacking it up trying to take advantage of foreigners, and now I speak with an American accent which gives me away." At ten euros I knew I could have been happy with the deal, but apparently we were not going to suffer a moral defeat.

TOO GOOD TO LAST?

Just when we were feeling settled and content, La Signora arrived on the scene seemingly determined to break our bubble. Reservations about her began to creep back in after we signed our agreement and Laura and I returned to Connecticut in March. We had engaged with her in a number of e-mail exchanges regarding the preparation of the dust- and clutter-encumbered property, some of which Laura was convinced went back to its creation some four hundred years ago. To appear objective, I asked one of the tour operator friends we had made, Simone, to rate it on a scale of one to ten in comparison with other *agriturismi* that he was familiar with from their tour business. He only gave the *borgo* a five, based on the dust and clutter and animals roaming freely about. We reported this in an e-mail to La Signora in hopes that she would address the issues before we returned and the season began. To soften the blow and assuage her fierce Roman pride, I added that no doubt his less than stellar rating had been influenced by the fact that unlike almost all other *agriturismi*, the *borgo* did not come with a pool.

A couple of days later, a response told us that our message had not only not really registered but had also not been well received. Much of the reply dealt with the deadly dangers of swimming pools, brimming with poisonous chemicals, and the inability of ignorant Americans to appreciate the beauty of pristine lakes like Bolsena. It took a couple of e-mails to settle her down. We realized we would have to walk gingerly when dealing with our partner but were not overly concerned since her stated plan was to spend the summer in Iceland painting.

TROUBLE IN PARADISE

Not so fast. For it seems that La Signora was having second thoughts about Iceland, which had recently been shrouded in a cloud of volcanic ash and was dominating the news, causing a major interruption to air traffic across much of Europe and gripping us with concern that expected visitors from the states would be forced to vacation elsewhere.

Sad to say that shortly after our May arrival back at the *borgo*, we saw what really lay beneath La Signora's patrician veneer. She just was not capable of partnering, and seemed to have a vacuum in that part of her mind where one usually finds conscience and concern for others. La Signora, all charm, advised us that she had taken the trouble to prepare a new and *proper* contract for us as she produced multiple legal-sized pages with typing front and back. I immediately smelled Italian bureaucracy, but beyond that I couldn't decipher the content. But Laura could. As she read it, the expression on her face slowly changed from a look of incredulousness to one of red hot seething anger.

Our so-called partner seemed to have forgotten all that we had agreed on before we forked over a healthy fistful of euros as our deposit back in March. The new document, which she declared to be a *proper contract*, only vaguely concealed in bureaucratic legalese, contained terms that scarcely reflected what La Signora originally presented to us and what we had so clearly agreed upon before any euros changed hands.

It seems this new document limited our use of the *borgo* to the *casale* and some but not all of the apartments. In addition, we were to be restricted in our right to walk on major portions of the grounds. It seems that her sons were expected to experience a sudden change of heart and would want to spend part of their summer at the place that we were initially told they had long ago forsaken. This made us especially anxious since we heard that one son, an actor, enjoyed throwing all-nighters with friends from his theater crowd.

La Signora had added that we were to be responsible for sharing in the potential repair of the septic system, which might not stand up because of our plans to bring an increasing number of guests to the *borgo*.

Laura was becoming more and more livid. Our dream was turning into a nightmare. We had made commitments to friends and family and to two art instructors and their students. I was thinking that Leona Helmsley has been replaced by a new Queen of Mean, and accordingly our wonderful summer was about to turn into a colossal disaster.

Laura did not try to contain her anger and told La Signora that it was obvious she had never made even the slightest go of running an *agriturismo* and could not begin to fathom what customer satisfaction was all about. A bit calmer, she added that we already had an agreement, which consisted of a single page both parties had executed in March, and we had no intentions of signing another document.

All the same, we began to brainstorm alternative locations, and we had the septic system at the *borgo* checked out by a local plumber. We received assurances that it was sound and that there was no need to anticipate a problem with it, but then he went on to volunteer that we might anticipate a problem with La Signora as many of the local townspeople have had. By then we had certainly figured it out on our own.

After checking other *agriturismi* in the regions for cost and availability, I began running numbers and concluded to Laura, "No way, dear. At this point no other place in the area can accommodate the art groups, and even if room does become available, maintaining our committed prices will create an incredible loss. We stand to lose face or money. Probably both."

Eventually La Signora relented in the face of a bit of compromise and concern that the new document could give us ammunition to take her to the *Guardie di Finanza*, the tax authorities. We agreed that she would hold one of the apartments for her own use, since her Iceland plans seemed to be in doubt, and we assured her that anytime her family or friends came when we were not fully occupied, there would be room for them.

We both felt she had taken us, and Laura was annoyed with me for giving ground. To add insult to injury, La Signora had treated her in a condescending manner. Tall, somewhat regal in appearance, and, in her own mind part of a grand aristocracy, she viewed the five foot tall Laura with disdain. She saw Laura as the vertically challenged butcher's daughter, a *popolana*, member of the plebeian mass, who had immigrated to America to tend other people's gardens.

Because of my limited knowledge of the language I didn't really grasp the offense. In Laura's eyes, I had failed to defend her honor. I understood that having La Signora around would have us continuously waiting for the other shoe to drop, but I was so taken with life in Italy and deeply concerned about the commitments we had made to people who had planned their vacations at the *borgo*. I reluctantly concluded I had no choice but to play the role of peacemaker. To dig in would have run the risk of losing it all. But by not digging in and pushing back more aggressively, I had put the promise of a serene time in romantic Italy at risk.

And so with a precarious peace where both La Signora and Laura were concerned, there was no choice but to take the bull by the horns and put the place in order. With perseverance, euros and tremendous help from Maria, we turned the place upside down and inside out. We transformed the *borgo* into what we believed a proper *agriturismo* ought to look like. This entailed several trips to Viterbo to purchase patio furniture, kitchen supplies, fans, and eventually sheets and blankets, repellents, an espresso machine, and cleaning supplies.

"This is really starting to cost," Laura posited. I could see the anger welling up.

"Remember, dear, that we share profits not total revenues. The furniture belongs solely to us and I am keeping track of all our expenses. Some belong to the business, but others are for our benefit, including friends and family when they come over to visit," I responded.

"So what are you planning to do with *our* furniture when we return to Connecticut at the end of the season?" I could tell that Laura had suffered a hurt that she could not easily get over.

When things seemed in order and La Signora had returned to Rome, Laura and I, feeling a somewhat shaky sense of relief, left for a short trip to London to meet some friends, who had invited us to join them for the Royal Ascot, the premier event of the English horse racing season. We had just enough time before our first guests were scheduled to arrive. Last summer, La Signora had taken a booking for a group of wedding guests who would be visiting from other parts of Italy and Germany.

THE FIRST GUESTS AND THE NIGHTMARE RESUMES

We returned from London eagerly to await the first set of guests, the aforementioned wedding party. All the rooms and apartments but one had been given the finishing touches. The bedrooms got a final once over dusting and featured the bedding that La Signora had provided and even made up herself. With Maria, we made sure the bathrooms were carefully supplied with the necessary toiletries and all the fixtures were functioning properly. As the designated breakfast guy, I made sure the kitchen was stocked with coffee and milk for cappuccino, fresh fruit and fruit juices. In the morning I would make a run to the bakery for fresh bread and some pastries. We were ready for business with our best foot forward.

At least that was what I thought at the time.

The one apartment we had not touched was the one that La Signora had been using in accordance with our compromise, but because of the size of the wedding party, the plan was for her to bring the key up from Rome and make it available for a late arriving guest and spend the night at a friend's place in town.

Hours after the first guests had checked in and left for dinner, we were still awaiting the arrival of La Signora and the key to the last apartment. We were a little anxious, but she finally arrived and opened the apartment just before the last guest arrived. The others came back from dinner, and she was holding court. Laura and I, her business partners, who with Maria had done all the work except make up those beds, were, like Maria, relegated to the role of staff, so we turned in for the night to be fresh for the morning's breakfast.

We awoke early only to be greeted by a couple of angry guests who wanted us to know that they had not been able to sleep a wink. One was busy on his cell phone trying to make arrangements for alternative lodgings. Others were angrily touting their grievances. It was obviously difficult for Laura to sort through the emotions and take in the cause of their anger, let alone translate for me. They would constantly interrupt her when she tried. Finally we got to the essence of the matter.

The guest from La Signora's apartment found it overwhelmed with bugs and had to leave in the middle of the night. He crashed with two of the girls staying in one of the bedrooms in the *casale*. Additionally, the guests in one of the *casale* bedrooms found the mattress smelling of cat urine. Eventually La Signora arrived. We were mortified. She was not. But she was concerned about them leaving and the lost revenue. A very loud three-way argument ensued, packed with emotion. The unhappy guests, having now made alternative arrangements, wanted their euros for the remaining night returned. La Signora argued that they were not entitled to any refund, while Laura apologized and rightly proclaimed our innocence with regard to the offending conditions.

Eventually La Signora relented and as the guests turned to leave she summoned up her patrician charm and incredulously bid them to recommend the *borgo* to their friends. They shot us a puzzled look and left.

"Not exactly a good start," I said to Laura who was too annoyed to reply at first but then woefully reiterated all we had done to prepare for our first guests. All but check the beds that La Signora, the cat lover, had made, and the apartment she had cleaved off in the agreement for her own use.

So that was the afternoon when we purchased the sheets. On our drive to and from the linen store we gave each other pep talks. "From now on ALL the preparation will be in our hands. No more embarrassing fiascos like this morning. We understand customer service," I preached.

Laura agreed but was having a hard time letting go of the morning's experience. She couldn't get over La Signora's behavior.

"Try to forget it. She'll be going back to Rome soon, and if I understood correctly she still has some kind of plan for Iceland where the cold climate should match her true personality."

Later in the day La Signora caught Laura, still in a forlorn mood, sitting out under the pergola and handed her an envelope containing our share of the one night's lodgings. Not half as per our agreement but 25% with the explanation that she had been the one to find those guests. Laura wanted to add that she had also been the one to drive them off, but wisely decided that it was not worth the effort.

That afternoon La Signora left again for Rome, but only after drawing Laura into one of the storage rooms to spend several hours taking her through an inventory of linens, all of which still had to be around at the end of the season. We heaved a deep sigh of relief when her car finally pulled through the gate after she bid us to be sure and lock it after her.

As summer approached and more guests visited, she seemed to make it a point to drive up from Rome in order to personally collect the bill. On one occasion, when she arrived only to learn that the guests had already left she exclaimed, "What, they left without paying?"

"No, they paid me. Here is your half." It made me pause and reflect. Was such behavior on her part simply the product of life in a society bereft of trust? I thought back to a confidence shared by an older Italian gentleman who told me that when filing his taxes he customarily divides his income by three.

"Why three?" I had asked.

"Because the government multiples what you report by two."

TO SEE OURSELVES AS OTHERS SEE US

One thing about living in another land is that you begin to see your world differently. I began to see my world through the eyes of Italians. I have always thought my vision of America to be fairly nonparochial. After all, business travel brought me to many countries, many times. And for many years, I have been married to an Italian born and raised wife. I take much of my news from British media. But talking with people here in Italy gave me an entirely new perspective on life on this planet.

I have already mentioned our meeting with the young *carabiniere* whose impression of American police was that they simply shoot away their problems. Frankly, it is hard for me to tell how serious his comments were, but I am pretty sure that many if not most Italians I met were ready to beatify our former president Barack Obama for singlehandedly fixing American healthcare with the passage of Obamacare. No longer will Italians have visions of Americans left dying in the streets because they cannot afford health insurance. On more than one occasion, upon learning we were American, an Italian volunteered to trade their "in again out again" prime minister Silvio Berlusconi for Barack Obama. I don't know whether their motivation was mostly an admiration for President Obama or a frustration with their prime minister, who once when asked if he was a faithful spouse, attempted a virtuous countenance and replied, yes, that he *frequently* was.

It seems to me that Italians expect much from their government. It is almost like the sense of dependency a small child has on his or her mother. And yet there seems to be little confidence, much cynicism and certainly little respect where government is concerned. Even humor has its place, as in the rumored story of then Prime Minister Craxi's visit to London, where he was hosted by the queen. As the story goes, the queen escorted him in a horse-drawn carriage. All was going well, when one of the horses broke wind with a booming resonance. With a royal concern for proper decorum, the queen turned to the prime minister and offered an apology, to which he is said to have replied that the apology wasn't necessary, for he thought it came from the horse.

But what really astonished me was that some Italians believed that America was to blame for the worldwide economic crisis that affected them. For as long as I can remember, Italians have managed to successfully and rather nonchalantly live well beyond their national means. So what if ratios of GDP and public debt are way out of whack? The wine is plentiful, the food arguably the world's best (and the most prevalent and endearing topic of conversation) and their fashion is world renowned. Life is good and things can always be put off until tomorrow.

But then something went terribly wrong. Americans had the audacity to adopt a lifestyle that Italians considered to be particularly their own. Americans, too, began to live significantly beyond their means, and this created a housing bubble that eventually burst with global ramifications.

And so, because of America's lack of fiscal discipline, Italians had to suck it up and cut 24 billion euro from their budget. Government employees would have to forego salary increases, public programs were delayed and the tax rates that the highest earners manage to never pay anyway were increased. The program had bipartisan support and was given the title "The Maneuver." I think it is a certainty that most found a way to create a maneuver of their own.

For the Italians I have met so far do not lack ingenuity. Take Gianpiero for instance. He owns and operates an *agriturismo* on a dozen or so acres that overlook Lake Bolsena. Initially the property simply functioned as a *fattoria* or farm, but then farming income began to decline. Just as manufacturing in the north of Italy found it difficult to compete with Asia, farms here began to lose market to Africa and other parts of the planet. Gianpiero found that it did not pay to plant his entire vineyard. Labor costs made it difficult to compete with growers in Chile. The yield from olive groves paled in comparison to younger economies, where trees were more systematically placed for mechanized pruning and picking. So he did what so many enterprising farmers across Italy have done. He converted part of the property into an *agriturismo*. Now he enjoys a government subsidy to facilitate the transition, and visitors from all over can come enjoy Gianpiero's lovely surroundings, breathe in the fresh air and enjoy the authentic cuisine and simple sulfite-free wines. And taking a page from Tom Sawyer, if they wished they could even pay him to help with the farm work.

Only now he faces a new problem. Visitors are not coming at the pace they once did. Gianpiero attributes it to the economy, but perhaps there is a bit of a "been there, done that" attitude as well. Then there is the demographic issue. Italy, even more than the rest of Europe, is failing to replace its population. So what can a farmer turned hospitality professional do? Gianpiero has the answer and it lies in the demographics. Turn the *agriturismo* into a home for the elderly.

In time, no doubt he will turn synergistic and convert the grape arbors into grave sites. And of course as it is with the conversion to an *agriturismo*, he would expect the government to subsidize each phase.

FOR NOW LIFE IS GOOD

But for all the concerns, life in Farnese was still good. We dined out in one of Farnese's three restaurants. That night, I honestly think I had the best pasta I have ever tasted, along with an amazing *antipasto* of zucchini, pear, pecorino, and *pignoli* (pine nuts) followed by a huge assortment of cheese and a bottle of spectacular wine from a neighboring village of Gradoli. It was indeed high end dining, yet dinner for the two of us ran the equivalent of about 78 USD.

I knew for sure that I was living the life in the Italy I had imagined. And nothing was dull. While every day since our arrival had its share of pleasure, after just a couple of weeks without La Signora around we started to experience a real sense of serenity. Since it was still a bit early for visitors to come to the b*orgo*, Laura and I had the entire place to ourselves. We set up housekeeping in what we considered to be the best apartment, which served as a base for day trips throughout the area. One day it would be the twenty-minute journey to the lake and the Paradise Beach Club. Another day we simply drove the scenic roads through lower Tuscany. Some trips were related to the business such as the trip to The Drink Store, a discount store where we stocked up on bottled water and my favorite Italian beers, while others were just to see the countryside. And there were days we just hung about the property enjoying the time together. Those days when we were not busy entertaining or enjoying the company of guests, or dealing with our so-called partner, were like a spectacular second honeymoon. We had so much time to enjoy one another's company. Time that was often hard to come by during our career years.

We enjoyed fantastic food, whether prepared with fresh vegetables, cheeses and olive oil at the *borgo* or in one of a half-dozen restaurants in Farnese or along the shores of Lake Bolsena, nearly always dining al fresco. There is something about dining outdoors that seems to further enhance the flavor of even the best prepared meals.

The countryside and weather could not be more ideal. There is something unique about the sun in Italy. It isn't just Tuscany, although the border is only a ten-minute drive from Farnese, but all throughout the region there is something special, yet hard to describe. Maybe it is a warmth as opposed to being hot, although the temperatures do climb, and during the stretch from about one in the afternoon to around four thirty the heat of the day curtails activity. The stores close and traffic essentially stops, but we don't think of it as hot. At least not in the way it gets hot at home in the northeast United States. Maybe it's the lack of humidity. Or perhaps it's the constant breeze up from the Med or sometimes from the mountains to the north. For this is the true Mediterranean climate, peaceful, warm, mellow.

Mornings, apart from an early morning jaunt into town for a cappuccino and to catch up on the local happenings, were often spent meandering through the back fields, "hectares," as I called them. We marveled at the olive trees and watched as the blossoms turned to tiny berries and eventually began to show themselves as definitely olives. We compared the different sizes and types. Laura was becoming quite good at that and had learned from Domenico, who would come by to care for them and who would eventually harvest them, just what the right blend of the various olives was that go into formulating the unrivaled color, texture, and flavors. We had become olive oil partisans. No other country's oil can rival that of Italy. And despite the myriad claims, no region in Italy can produce an oil that matches that of the local Canino olive.

The *borgo* property contained a small grape arbor, although grapes were not tended to and were not to become fine wine. From rummaging about in one of the barns, we discovered old vats, wine casks and a large press all left over from days gone by when the property supported subsistence farming. Nowadays we could look forward to picking the grapes in the fall, but only for eating them. The property's real treasure was an abundance of fruit trees. The apricots ripen first, followed by two varieties of plums. Next come the cherries, followed by the peaches, pears, blackberries and ultimately the figs, in two varieties. Ah, the figs. There was an abundance, and they went well with prosciutto or on bread to make a fresh juicy "fig newton."

We learned that the key to enjoying produce is to go with the season. Enjoy what ripens, and before you have your fill, the next delight will be ready for picking. In truth, we learned this early in our stay in what proved to be an embarrassing moment for Laura.

I had some bloodwork done at a hospital in Pitigliano during our stay, and the analysis suggested a slight iron deficiency. Laura believes that every effect has a cause and when that effect manifests itself in the form of any kind of bodily ailment, there has to be a natural cure. So her simple solution was to feed me some spinach. We checked out both markets in town, but no spinach. On the third attempt at the market in neighboring Valentano, she mildly mentioned her frustration. "This is the third market I have visited and none of them have any spinach."

At that the grocer dressed her down. "How could you possibly be seeking to buy spinach when it is out of season and so many other fine vegetables are being picked each one of these early summer days?" The grocer shook his head in disbelief, and my embarrassed wife walked out reminded that we were in Italy, where one goes with the flow or in this case the growing season. And once you accept that, it is hard to beat.

SOME SERENITY, BACK TO THE GRAPES

La Signora returned, counted all the linens, photographed the furnishings, disconnected the phone so no one would run up her phone bill (How could potential guests call to make reservations?), and headed off to Iceland for a spell.

Before she left she seemed to feel the need to put the staff in its proper place, which meant belittling Laura. Because she did so in Italian and because I had taken to avoiding her as much as possible, most of it passed by me. La Signora had successfully stirred the pot leaving behind more than a little tension in the air. Once again Laura's frustration settled on me since by being silent and often unavailable, I failed to take her side.

Chagrined, I found myself again wondering if our Italian dream was destined to become a nightmare. And I wondered if our Iceland bound partner planned to take a plane or a broomstick.

With La Signora gone, we could now fully enjoy the facility along with all the Tuscia region had to offer, while focusing on building some business. To put the bruises aside, we turned to the *vino*. Towns like Montalcino and Montepulciano and words like Brunello and Super Tuscan come to mind when Americans think of Italian wines, and well they should. Neither Laura nor I claim to be any kind of connoisseur. The truth is that both Laura and I enjoy light but rich flavored wines that we can drink at both lunch and dinner without succumbing to headaches or the feeling of "wish we had not" the next day. Another way of looking at it is finding "drinkable" wines that complete a meal and do not leave us feeling the need to mortgage the house to cover our costs.

Well, the Tuscia region was just the place for us. With only two exceptions, the wines we tried—and we tried many— met or exceeded our expectations. I confess to having spent as much as fifteen euros for a splendid bottle of wine from Gradoli once, when Laura and I celebrated at Pepe Nero, the white tablecloth restaurant on the shores of Lake Bolsena. For the most part we enjoyed a Tuscan red from Pitigliano and a white from Farnese itself at costs ranging between 65 and 85 euro cents a liter. Of course we purchased in multi liter jugs and made it a point to return the empty jug to Giovanni's, where we did most of our purchasing.

An interesting fact about Pitigliano, the closest Tuscan town, is that it is the home of one of Italy's first ghettos. The ghetto remains today, and coupled with it is the fact that the wine from the cooperative is produced by the Jews of the town and presumably meets kosher standards, for much of it is shipped to Israel. It is light, smooth and flavorful with just one catch. Because it does not contain sulfites, you cannot let it sit for long without souring. And so dutifully, we made every reasonable effort to make fast work of any jug once opened.

I must add that we were quite successful at that. Whether *pranzo* or *cena* (lunch or dinner), wine complements the meal. And one of the most wonderful things about the meal is the lingering. In Italy it is traditional to take your time and savor every aspect of the meal. And when the food is finally finished, linger longer over a second glass of wine, or perhaps a third. Add easy conversation, the most frequent topic of which is usually food, and you have the ideal Italian meal.

A MOST UNUSUAL SHOPPING EXPERIENCE

With all of the eating and drinking, my plan was to do some cycling on a fairly regular basis to ensure that there would not be more of me returning to the states at the end of the season. What I enjoy about riding a bicycle is aerobic exercise combined with the opportunity to explore, and Farnese and its surrounding hillsides measured up on both counts. The scenery is spectacular and with hardly any stretches of level terrain, the heart really gets pumping.

Bringing my bike over from the states seemed unduly complicated (as it turned out, coming over with tennis rackets proved challenging enough). Our plan was to purchase or rent a few bikes locally. Taking a logical approach, we googled a few bike shops in the vicinity. None of them were very close, so we postponed checking them out in favor of first locating a boat rental on Lake Bolsena. We headed to the marina in Capodimonte, the closest lakeside town. As we were parking the car near the marina, a rather striking senior gentleman approached on a smart looking bicycle. Laura bid him a *buongiorno*, good morning, to which he smiled and bid her the same. She admired his bike and asked if he knew of any local source for renting or purchasing a bicycle. He replied affirmatively, motioning toward a nearby house and let loose a volley of Italian so fast and furious that it was totally beyond my understanding. Laura said something to him that also went right by, and after he let loose another loud and long barrage, she turned to me and said, "We are going with him. Bicycles are his passion."

We crossed the street. Our leader was still talking loudly and nonstop. In front of the house we made introductions. He introduced himself as Costantino, and in turn Laura introduced the two of us, explaining that we were from America and that being American I unfortunately did not speak Italian. This seemed to strike him as odd, and he raised his voice a few octaves and seemed to repeat his earlier remarks, which only added to my confusion. I turned to Laura for an explanation. Laura was beaming but unable to get a word in edgewise. Costantino had thrust open the garage door and at once I understood. Alongside his motor scooter there were no fewer than twenty bicycles. Costantino turned to me and took on an authoritative manner. Still speaking in capital letters, he directed me toward one particular bike. I told him as best I could that it was a fine looking bike, which sparked another loud barrage. Capital letters and exclamation points, even. I must have looked puzzled, as he raised his tone a few more decibels and repeated himself several times while Laura interjected, "Try it out."

I took the handlebars, but Costantino stopped me and proceeded to take a wrench in hand and adjust the seat. Costantino was hardly taller than five foot Laura, so the seat was raised about a foot before I got on and took off.

Five rides on five bikes later, with much booming instruction from Costantino, we settled on two mountain bikes, one for me and the other for Jake, our grandson, who would be joining us from Brooklyn to help out when school finished. The bikes could also be used for any other visitor who might have an interest in seeing the countryside while sitting atop two wheels. They proved appropriate for the terrain, and at a cost of 130 euro total, paid for themselves several times over.

With my trusty yellow steed I was able to ride the countryside early on with Joe Lazaroff, my friend who came over from Connecticut, and later with our new friend Liam O'Brien, who proved to be an excellent local guide when our son Fran and my friend Mike joined us with their families later in the summer. Probably the most memorable ride occurred on a day when I was laboring to keep up with Liam, who was 38 years old, and Fran and Mike, a pair of triathletes in their early forties. As we approached one hill, Liam and Fran geared down, slowing to wait for me while Mike, probably imagining himself in a triathlon, burst ahead and over the crest of the hill. In time we too reached the top only to find Mike on the other side, fully enmeshed in a flock of sheep. Mike looked a bit nervous, but no more so than the sheep.

HERDS OF CATS

If you've traveled to Italy, you know that cats abound there, notably in Rome where they're something of a tourist attraction. Located in the heart of the ancient city, many stray and abandoned cats find shelter amid old Roman temples that date back almost two and a half millenia. The shelter is called Torre Argentina. There, seven days a week, volunteers from around the world feed, clean, and care for the cats. It's even possible for tourists to adopt a cat there and bring it home to their own country. The cats are all vaccinated, dewormed, and spayed or neutered. To make sure the cats are going to loving families, the people at the shelter insist on interviewing prospective adopters. The cats aren't pedigreed, of course, but they're authentic *veri gatti romani*—genuine Roman cats.

In Farnese the cat population is feral and analogous to the deer population in some suburban areas of the United States. They can be adorable creatures—and nuisances. Like their big-cat cousins in Africa, they live in the wild. Their lifespan can't be very long, since the environment they live in is ruled by the survival of the fittest, or perhaps the luckiest.

Nuisances or not, feral cats can be useful. This is particularly true around farms, where they ward off mice, rats, and even snakes. The cats at the *borgo*—unlike so many American cats—were slender and lithe. I found it fascinating to watch them tiptoeing through our fields, stalking their prey. I admired their athleticism as they leapt through the air and pounced upon their hapless victims. Even so, they presented a major problem. For one thing, there were just so many of them. One summer morning we counted fourteen.

For another thing, some of them found hunting inside the *casale* or the apartments was easier and more rewarding than hunting in the fields. Why chase down a gecko in the fields when you could wander through an open door, bound up to the kitchen counter, and feast on all kinds of goodies?

Cats aren't dumb. They appreciate Italian cuisine. That was once demonstrated to Laura and me when La Signora was preparing a meal. As she was chopping up a chicken, a cat leapt onto the counter, made a beeline to the lasagna, scooped up a morsel, and began devouring it. Except for a delighted cry of "*Micio!*" (tomcat), La Signora paid no attention to him. Needless to say, Laura and I took dinner in town that night.

In the past after such events, La Signora had been known to leave for Rome, locking the villa where she'd been staying. When she returned to the *casale* a week or more later, she found that several starving *gatti* had been locked inside it. Chagrined, she made it a point to lavish food on them. Perhaps it eased her conscience. It certainly reinforced the cats' belief that fine dining was still available in the villa. Her concern for the poor creatures overrode any concern for what they may have done to the *casale* when trapped inside it.

So while I did admire the creatures, I had to devise a way to keep them outside at all times where they could live their lives as true farm cats. On the surface that seemed easy enough but the reality proved different. The door had a bolt spring lock, which would only completely close when someone used a key. When not locked and left even a tiny bit ajar, curious or hungry cats could, with nose or paw, push the door open enough to enter. Once inside they would head straight for the kitchen. Or if the kitchen window was opened to let in the cooling breeze, our cat friends could scale the five foot wall and enjoy a shortcut through the window directly to whatever culinary delight might be in whatever stage of preparation. If the shortcut wasn't available, cats could always take the long way around through a hall, bathroom or bedroom window, take their pickings from the kitchen and scamper away with it to some hiding place under a chair or sofa. For the *borgo's* fine felines, life in Italy could be better than good. But clearly their behavior had to be modified and the burden fell to me.

"No cats will outsmart this marketing exec turned inn keeper," I said to Joe Lazaroff, our first visitor from home where he and his wife, Kim Pendergast, were the proud owners of two beautiful Persian house cats.

"Cats are pretty resourceful," he responded respectfully.

The initial line of defense I set up involved a bamboo screen hung in front of the door. No more than ten minutes after I hung it, a little grey rascal pawed it open so she and a mate could scamper in. Not deterred, I chased them down and sent them out and locked the door. Then Laura and I drove to Viterbo and purchased a heavier hanging curtain for the doorway and a super soaker water gun.

The new curtain clung tightly to the doorframe, and it briefly appeared that I had the problem licked until a slight gust of wind blew the curtain sideways and the young grey's head peeked through the opening. Time for the second line of defense. I grabbed the super soaker and fired a volley into the air simulating a rain shower. That worked. Cats in retreat! But my sense of accomplishment only lingered for a moment as I realized my stay in Italy would not be all that enjoyable if I had to spend my days posted on guard duty.

Then Laura read on the Internet that cats disliked lavender and, just coincidentally, she thought it would be nice to attend a lavender festival in one of the neighboring towns, planned for that weekend. Their promotion suggested lavender fields that were on a par with Provence, which turned out to be gross hyperbole. And it further turned out to be the hottest day of the summer, with the festival site under the noonday sun. Not a leaf of shade could be found. I didn't find the lavender drinks cool or refreshing as promoted, let alone tasty. I grumped that the bunches of lavender and little lavender filled pillows Laura purchased for anti-cat measures set us back some thirty euros.

We returned to the *borgo* and strategically positioned the new deterrents. In less than ten minutes we learned that our cats had nothing at all against lavender.

And so on to the next plan. Joe had mentioned that cats were uncomfortable on surfaces that did not allow them to gain a firm footing. With that in mind, I went to the closest building supply house and purchased sheets of wire fencing, which I laid out in overlapping two-inch blocks in front of the doorway. Now I had a Maginot Line, and an entryway that was beginning to resemble the town dump.

That, combined with screening I laboriously tacked to the windows, proved somewhat successful in keeping them out, but their population was increasing. "We've a rash of teen pregnancies," I reported to Laura and, even though they didn't often make it into the house, they developed the annoying habit of loitering just beyond my barricades. Laura suggested that we try feeding them in an established place far from the *casale*, and that was what eventually did the trick. By then our fourteen-year-old grandson Jake had joined us, and together Jake and I set up a cat dining facility in the stone barn farthest from the *casale*.

It became Jake's responsibility to feed the pesky felines, and soon a daily ritual developed. At about seven each morning the cats clustered outside the second story window of the room Jake slept in. If he failed to appear at the window by about five after seven there would be an annoying chorus to rouse him. Soon he would emerge from the *casale* carrying several cans of cat food and take his place at the head of a parade to the farthest out barn where he set down breakfast. Content, the herd hung out there until early evening when they would once again make their way to the *casale* and announce to Jake that the dinner hour was upon them.

We had managed to solve the problem of the cats while Jake also learned a lesson in basic economics. For once he began to feed them, the cats all became socialists. No longer did they hunt geckos and rodents in the field. Why would they have to earn their keep when the government, in the form of Jake, was expected to take care of them? And so they became fat and lazy. But they never stopped reproducing. As for Jake, he developed a better understanding of macroeconomics, explaining that cats are no different from people and socialism just does not work.

A SERIOUSLY BAD DAY

But I am getting ahead of myself. One of the great joys of the *borgo* experience was spending significant time with Jake, who is the oldest of our six grandchildren. Numero uno, as we like to say. When we first considered the idea of taking on the *agriturismo*, we thought about the potential opportunity to give the grandkids a new cultural experience. We suggested to our daughter, Monica, that Brooklyn-based Jake might be enriched by spending a summer in a small village in Italy, helping with our project. Monica has had a lifelong love affair with her mother's homeland. Apart from Laura, she is the best Italian speaker in the family, having spent the summer of her tenth year in Rome with her *zio* and *zia*, (aunt and uncle), her eleventh year of high school in Rome and a stretch as a teaching assistant with Dartmouth College in Siena. Jake himself had begun to feel that New York was the center of the universe and nothing outside of it really counted for much. This was a perfect opportunity for him to expand his horizons. But raising a teenager, even one who excelled at school and avoided trouble can be challenging for parents, and as we learned, for grandparents as well.

For me, the cats were merely an irritant. The day Jake was scheduled to arrive had more of the makings of a true disaster. It was a first class fright and surprisingly it had nothing to do with La Signora. It happened the day we were scheduled to meet Jake at the Leonardo da Vinci airport in Rome.

There was more than a little bit of anxiety among the female members of the family because "cheapskate" me scheduled his flight with a stopover through Dublin. Yes, the very same Dublin airport where Laura was nabbed as a potential agent of terror. Jake was nearly fourteen and pretty smart, so I was not concerned, nor was he when he learned that he would be changing planes in Dublin. He understood the wisdom of taking advantage of the significant savings Aer Lingus offered on flights to Rome, so long as you could accept a change of aircraft in Dublin. But his mother and Laura, his *nonna*, did not.

By the day of his arrival, I had begun to feel like an old hand at Rome's Leonardo da Vinci Airport. I had learned where I could find parking and easily locate the appropriate arrival point where visitors, who had just cleared customs could be tearfully embraced by their Italian loved ones. But when an hour had passed by, and the flight was reported to have landed, and there was no sign of our grandson, my confidence began to wane. I started to get a bit sweaty. And it got hard to look Laura straight in the eye.

As one hour became nearly two, we began to take action beyond pacing back and forth in front of the exit area. We positioned Laura's sister at the gate as a sentry while we scurried about the airport looking for answers. At less than five feet tall, Adriana couldn't see over anyone's head, but as a loving aunt and true Italian, she elbowed her way to the front of the crowd, determined not to relinquish her post until the rascal appeared. Laura went to chase down any and all authorities who would give her the time of day. A tough assignment, indeed.

I began to sweat more and lamented the morning in April or May when I did the Internet search to find the best fares, accepting a change of planes in Ireland. I paced and sweated as two hours passed. Reluctantly, I called Monica back in Brooklyn. It felt like the toughest call of my life. All I could think was: failed father, failed husband and failed grandfather.

"No, Dad. I haven't heard from him. The plane must be delayed. No worries. He has his cell and will call when they land." But I could feel her reaction changing to concern as I explained that the plane had landed two hours ago and unsaid, I knew she was thinking, "Dad, why are you such a cheapskate? He could have been put on a direct flight." My anxiety and imagination began to get the best of me. I had visions of him having bailed out in Dublin, sitting in a pub off of O'Connell Street. Or maybe he had joined the IRA.

Finally we had a breakthrough. Laura called my cell from somewhere within the labyrinth of the airport. "Jake was detained by immigration."

"What? Do they think he is a terrorist? Was he carrying a tennis racket?" He wasn't, nor as it turns out his passport, which had been lost somewhere between Dublin and Rome. Laura was in tears. She saw him but was dismissed by the immigration authorities without any means of resolving the mess Jake was in, which was now also quite a mess for me. I recalled the Tom Hanks movie, where unable to enter the new country and unable to return to his country of origin, he lived for a year in the airport. But there was no humor in this situation. At least not at the time. The passport guy was Mussolini reincarnated, round shaved head and all. I pushed past a couple of his flunkies and made my way into his office, flashed my American passport and demanded satisfaction. I got a response in Italian that I did not completely understand other than, "I am not going to speak to you in English, and while you are at it, American, screw off." I wanted to strangle him by one of the three gold chains he wore around his fat neck as he confiscated my passport. Penitently, Laura interceded and the guy, having asserted his power, gave a millimeter. "You can call those incompetents at the American embassy and see if they will grovel and then issue a new passport," he grudgingly offered.

I called the embassy, and they were polite and concerned. They offered to call Mussolini and take responsibility for Jake. More time passed and finally Jake, who was nonplussed by the whole affair, was released with the proviso that he go immediately to the embassy to get a temporary passport. The embassy gave me instructions, including the fact that this was one of those unfortunate days when Rome was experiencing a transit strike. I would have to drive through the heart of the city to the embassy on the Via Veneto in my trusty Peugeot chariot.

And so we drove into the morass of Roman traffic. Without public transit it seemed that every Roman had taken to car or scooter. We circled the Colosseum and passed Castel Sant'Angelo. Along the Tiber we caught the dome of St. Peter's in the background. Up shifting. Down shifting. It seemed like a giant game of dodge-a-car.

"Check that out, Jake," I said, but he was sound asleep in the back seat. The embassy stayed open beyond normal closing, and Jake and Laura were greeted at the door like visiting congressmen, while Adriana and I went for a coffee and a beer, respectively. The embassy came through and we all headed to Farnese. I was still a bit shaky at the wheel but at least I had stopped sweating. And we had our Jake safe and sound.

BACK FROM ICELAND

La Signora's stay in Iceland only lasted a little over a week. She came up from Rome more frequently and stayed in one of the apartments for longer and longer stays. Laura suggested to her that it seemed like an unusual thing to do, given that she had complained that coming to the *borgo* was burdensome, and that we had paid her rent for the use of the property. This seemed to strike her fancy as she laughed and replied, "You didn't really expect me to spend the summer in Rome, did you?"

I guess we naively thought she really would stay in Iceland, but we realistically understood that she would lose face if seen hanging out in Rome during the summer, when all respectable Romans, even those with the most meager of funds, would be heading to the beaches or the mountains. It seemed to this Yank that for the Italian psyche, nothing is more important than saving face.

AND IF THE CATS DON'T GET YOU, THIS WILL

Just as I was feeling good about having solved the cat problem and witnessing Jake's lesson in nature, La Signora arrived from Rome with three dogs in tow and declared that they would have to stay.

This led to an unpleasant conversation. My half in English; La Signora's half in Italian. And I half prevailed. La Signora returned to Rome the next day with two of the dogs leaving the mangiest of the lot behind to join Fiona, the farm dog, on the property she had *rented to us*.

Not long after, she returned with a chicken in tow. But the hen, which was soon joined by a second, was not a problem, although neither produced any eggs. While neither the mangy dog nor the chickens were much of a problem, it seems that in Laura's mind, my willingness to compromise was becoming a problem. My motivation was avoiding a vendetta—no need to make this situation any more difficult.

"Try to put it aside, hon," I would say. But to the former Marialaura Ferrini, La Signora had crossed the Rubicon and as her committed life partner, I was duty bound to mount a counterattack. Hadn't her fierce Roman pride been constantly compromised?

And so from that point on I realized my efforts as peacemaker wouldn't do even if they did succeed.

Fortunately La Signora returned to Rome and so my "call to arms" was put on hold for a time. Now we could fully enjoy the facility along with all the Tuscia region had to offer while focusing on building some business. But first we had another issue to contend with if our guests and in fact we ourselves were to be truly comfortable staying at the borgo.

The chickens were not really a problem, and we had learned to live with the dogs, but as the weather grew warmer we began to encounter another challenge. Since the *borgo* shared Farnese and its surrounding hills with the sheep, goats, cows, horses and an occasional donkey, it also attracted a large number of flies. We first attempted to meet the challenge in the most ecologically sound and traditional mode: flyswatters and rolls of fly paper. They worked, but not effectively enough on days when the sun was strong and the wind was weak. However, if we had licked the cats, surely we could handle the flies. Laura picked up a spray from the hardware store, but after a couple of days we had just as many flies and an empty spray can. There had to be a better solution, so I started to ask around. Liam commiserated with me and volunteered that the repellent in the blue can worked better than anything he had tried. Liam's wife Gabriella chimed in that when the flies came around, Liam would turn into a bit of a madman, running about the house spraying everywhere, everything, and, if they happened to be in the way, everyone in sight.

And so that evening on our way to dinner at Liam and Gabriella's we stopped at the hardware store and bought the repellent in the blue can. The women who ran the store commented that Liam had stopped by earlier and purchased the same thing, so we felt reassured that we had the correct repellent. When we arrived at Liam's, he announced that he had a gift for us and proceeded to produce a can of the repellent. The next morning we launched a two-fisted attack on the pesky creatures and pretty soon declared victory. We had defeated the cats and now the flies, but La Signora was a different story.

And before we knew it, La Signora was back, and with no guests to take care of for a few days we found it difficult to avoid her meddling and harping. We would busy ourselves with some local hikes and afternoons at the lake, but when we returned to the *borgo* she would soon enough be in our face about one thing or another. After two days of what I considered mental cruelty, I hit upon an idea.

"If she is not going to stay in Rome, then Rome is the place to be. And after all, apart from the short initial visit with your sister, you haven't had time to spend in your favorite city," I suggested to Laura. "It will be a diversion. A chance to get our minds off our nemesis."

Laura agreed. "I'll call my niece and see if by chance they have space available at the B&B." It turned out that they did, and so we went off to Rome for a few days.

Ale & Niki's Home is an eight-room bed and breakfast located in the heart of Rome. It is just a ten-minute walk to the Vatican. Finding our way there and locating a parking spot turned out to be challenging, but with a bit of missed directions and a few wrong turns, we eventually succeeded.

"Ciao Zia, Zio," greeted Niki, the older of the two sisters and lovelier than ever. Niki was now in her mid-twenties, which served to remind me once more how quickly the years had gone by. We caught up a bit over coffees and enjoyed a tour, peeking into some of the rooms that were open for the cleaning lady and observing the convivial manner with which Niki greeted guests in a variety of different languages.

After unpacking, we set off on the ten-minute walk to the Vatican, and after an hour or so crossed the Tiber and walked up the Aventine hill to view the Circus Maximus and the Rose Garden before enjoying lunch on the rooftop restaurant of Forty Seven Hotel. We were reacquainting ourselves with "the glory that was Rome from another day," to paraphrase Tony Bennett. As walkers, we caught most of the sights by foot, clocking nearly twenty thousand steps a day.

After stepping back into history, Laura and I checked out the latest fashions on the blocks of storefronts in Niki's neighborhood. One thing struck me about the latest contemporary fashion in female attire: emphasis was placed on the posterior. Not mentally engaged in Laura's attempts to match the appropriate gifts from Rome with potential recipients, I began to ruminate on the style of dress in fashion-conscious Italy. Thinking back to an earlier visit, I recalled the early adoption of the bikini and the emphasis on the cleavage in ordinary summer dress. I remembered how the church reacted back then. In an effort to promote modesty, women who displayed even a hint of their fairer physical attributes were forbidden to enter the premises. It became a real conflict and if church attendance is any measure of success, clearly the fashionable female won, for church attendance is not all that popular in Catholic Italy.

At about nine in the evening, having taken in a bunch of history and fashion, we headed to dinner at LUMA, the local *ristorante* around the corner from the B&B. The pastas there were all homemade and flash frozen, so they didn't lose their freshness. The wine was superb. Ready for rest, we returned to our spacious, smartly furnished room at our home away from home. It was both cozy and contemporary. No thoughts of La Signora for a couple of blissful days before heading back to Farnese and the *borgo* to greet a new set of guests.

LA FAMIGLIA, THE FAMILY

The days when the *nipoti*, or grandchildren, were with us were the highlight of the entire adventure. We are blessed with six. Jake is the oldest. His responsibilities here were to handle the garbage, help with setting the table and clearing after meals, and most importantly, herding the cats. When he began to exhibit an occasional bout of typical teenage ennui, I added to his responsibilities by instructing him to compose a page-long descriptions of the various attractions we visited. Once written, they were available to help other visitors plan their sightseeing trips.

We had struck a bargain. Jake would come to Farnese soon after school ended and assume his responsibilities in exchange for our providing him with a laptop when he started his first year of high school at Brooklyn Tech in the fall. Needless to say, Laura and I were overjoyed at the prospect of his company for a large chunk of the summer.

Before too long Jake was joined by his nearly eleven-year-old brother, Nick, and his seven-year-old sister, Grace. Jake, with his dark hair and complexion, had inherited a disproportionate share of Italian genes, while Nick owed his light skin and blue eyes to his dad's Danish and Swiss side. Grace was born in China and joined the family when she was nine months old. She began to exhibit an interest in fashion around her fifth or sixth birthday, which we think is why she, while proud of her Chinese heritage, wanted to be considered Italian even more than the boys.

The two boys and the young fashionista, along with our daughter Monica and her husband Pete, occupied one wing of the *casale*. The other wing of the *casale* was the temporary residence of our son, Francis, his wife, Michelle and their three little ones: Caroline, William and Thomas, ages seven, five, and three, respectively. The young California Coens took to life in Farnese like ducks to water. Caroline expressed a desire to live out her life in Italy. For a five-year-old, William showed a remarkable interest in the various historical sights we visited. I attributed that to his also having inherited a disproportionate collection of genes from Laura. I drew this conclusion when I first saw him as an infant, noting that the second toe on his right foot crossed over the third toe just as Laura's mother's had. My assessment was reinforced by the brightness of his dark brown eyes that an aunt on Michelle's side describes as "those chocolate chip eyes."

Thomas also took to Italy in an unusual manner for a three-year-old. After a couple of days in Farnese, Tommy determined that he had turned into a *cinghiale*, a wild boar, and as such delighted in running around the yard proclaiming his metamorphosis to all. In case we had doubts, he began snorting. The magic of Italy affects us in different ways.

What a delight it was to have them all with us, and although Laura and I lamented that our second daughter, Daniela, and her husband Allen were unable to join us because of work commitments, we found every moment with the family precious beyond description.

I got such pleasure at mealtime, looking down from my spot at the head of the table to the assemblage of friends and family sometimes numbering as many as eighteen. At dinnertime we assembled at the long table, and prior to Amabile serving, children and adults took turns announcing the highlight of their day. We were warmed whenever one of the children volunteered one aspect or another of our being together as an extended family, but equally pleased to hear a seven-year-old tell us it was learning about an Etruscan artifact or viewing a castle from medieval times. And no praise was spared when they commented on Laura's choice of menu and Amabile's cooking. At the end of these days I would usually doze off reveling in thoughts of the children and their joys at discovering all that Italy had to offer.

Then something disturbed me. Five-year-old William announced that he was getting bored with Italy and felt it time he return to California. This caused a stir as seemingly all at once everyone told him that he was not being reasonable, and anyway, since the rest of his family planned to stay another week, he would have to stay as well. Not to be deterred, William slung his backpack on his shoulder and headed toward the gate. Amid a cacophony of protests, he turned and announced that since Jake had been able to make the trip on his own, so too could he.

Someone countered, "But you will have to change planes in Dublin."

"I have my passport," he responded, glancing toward Jake before he turned again toward the gate. I didn't know what to do to stop him. But fortunately just as he was about to turn down the road, I awoke from my dream!

THE DAILYNESS OF LIFE: IT IS THE LITTLE THINGS

While La Signora posed a constant threat to our serenity, thankfully she was not there all the time and there were times when there were not any guests either. Those were delightful days, such as the especially warm day when we lunched on only a simple combination of melon and prosciutto, followed by a couple of small chunks of cheese, and finished off with a peach. These delights were accompanied by a glass of Italian bubbly known as prosecco. I was truly liberated from the "desk dining" I so often experienced pre-retirement. After lunch, we enjoyed some quiet time while I worked on my computer and frequently glanced up at Laura soaking up some vitamin D, while tending to the gardens in the midday heat, her petite bronze bod clad in only her bikini. I thanked God for this "small" favor.

There was entertainment to be found in a thousand little things that people do and say. I was amused by the elderly gentleman who, upon parking his Vespa, leaned down to smooth his hair in the tiny side mirror or the gentleman we bid "*buongiorno,*" only to receive a puzzled look in exchange and then a polite smile and "*grazie*," explaining that he forgot his hearing aid as he scampered back up the stairs to his house to get it.

A favorite of the town folks was Cecilia, one of the legion of flowery house dress attired senior women, whom we met one morning as we passed the cemetery on our way to our morning cappuccino. Cecilia made the nearly one mile trek from her apartment in town up the hill to the cemetery to visit the resting spot of her late husband. She made sure that the gravesite was clean for him and, when in season, the flowers were fresh. As we walked to town together, she lamented her loss, confiding to Laura how she missed him so. I wanted to console her and advise that time can heal all wounds, but before I had a chance, Laura asked her how long it had been since her dear husband departed. Sadly, she responded that it had been over five years. I decided to leave well enough alone. I thought, this is her life, this is what she does. Love has no time limits.

DANTE EVENED THE SCORE

We continued to meet many delightful characters. Another toward the top of the list was an octogenarian gentleman, who with his wife restored an ancient Etruscan fishing compound and planted a lovely garden. I cannot do justice to his description of how the early inhabitants, the Etruscans and then Romans, viewed eels as a great delicacy, as do many Italians today, who treasure the rich fatty meat.

The gentleman regaled us with his description of the eels' journey from Lake Bolsena, through the Marta River to the Mediterranean Sea, across the Atlantic and through the Gulf Stream to the Caribbean, where they spawned, and the enigma of their offspring's return to the lake. To capture the delicacy centuries ago, the Etruscans built an elaborate trap to intercept the eels' journey as they "returned" home to Lake Bolsena on this tributary of the Marta River.

We were told of the medieval Pope Gregory, I forget which one, who so prized the eels that he had a gargantuan feast prepared and dined on eel to great excess. It was reported that he would have his cook drop them in vats of wine, which both killed and pickled them. Later they were roasted and served in large quantities. He died in his sleep from overeating. Apparently, there is an inscription on his tomb suggesting that in the end the eels got their revenge. "The eels are glad that he is dead/And lies interred in his low bed," wrote Dante, who placed him in purgatory, which isn't necessarily the place you expect to find a pope.

HEALTH CARE ITALIAN STYLE

As if dealing with La Signora were not enough, I found my health now taking a turn for the worse. We dug into our medicine stash, but in just a couple of days it became clear that neither Laura's homeopathic remedies nor any of the over the counter stuff we brought over from the states seemed to be helping.

"No choice," Laura stated. "You are going to have to get acquainted with Italy's socialized medical system." One of our new friends advised us that the local general practitioner enjoyed a first class reputation, both within the town and in professional communities.

"If Terry needs him to, he can come to the *borgo*, or if possible you can visit him in his office," he offered.

"How can we get his phone number and schedule an office visit?" I asked.

This drew a puzzled look and he replied, "No appointment. Just be sure to get to his office early, sign in, and when your number comes up, it will be your turn to see him." Take a number? Just like at the deli counter or, this being Italy, just like taking a number at the post office, I thought.

"Should we expect to have to wait long?" asked Laura.

"Well, yes, but no problem. Just sign in and go out for a coffee. That is what everybody does," he reassured.

"Well, not this body," I said. "I am in no mood for a social occasion. I just need to get on the mend so I can deal with La Signora and the mess she is causing us."

So first thing in the morning, a good hour before the good doctor was scheduled to arrive on the scene, we hustled to his office and located the sign-in sheet, only to see that nineteen people were already ahead of us.

"There must be an epidemic," I told Laura, as I scanned the room expecting to find something akin to the emergency room at our local Connecticut hospital. But I could only see five or six people, and not a one of them struck me as appearing to be ill. In fact, they not only appeared quite healthy, but they also were so busy bantering about their number on the sign-in sheet that the whole waiting room resembled the buzz of a Bingo parlor.

"Che numero hai?" one of them inquired. What number are you?

"Venti," I responded, which means twenty. The whole room seemed to repeat it and with a shake of their collective heads advised that we better go for a coffee. I was in no mood for a coffee or anything else, save a chance to meet with the doctor, so when we did not get up and head to the Rokkabar, one well-intentioned soul sympathized, and advised us that she herself had been number 16 just two days past. Then the room erupted in a whole flurry of laughter and burst of Italian that went over my sorry head. After more than an hour went by, I noted that the list was being pared down very slowly.

"What number is in there now?" I inquired. No one responded, for all were busily engaged in one conversation or another. Finally someone looked my way.

"Cinque (five)," he responded. Just then, the door to the doctor's office opened and out strode the local healer, head down, looking neither left nor right.

"Emergency?" Laura inquired to no one in particular.

"No, no," echoed the now familiar chorus. "It is time for his coffee."

As the frustration grew, it seemed that I was hurting all the more and thought that some fresh air would help me. Feeling assured my turn would not come until maybe the good doctor had taken a second break, I dragged a chair out to the front of the building where I happened upon my new friend Alonzo. Alonzo had spent the eighteen years after his fifty-fifth birthday traveling five continents in a motor home before settling into retirement in Farnese, but that is another story.

"What are you doing here, Terry?" he inquired. I explained my condition including that I was number twenty, at which he shook his head, let out a sigh, and advised me to go for a coffee, before giving me his take on visits to the doctor.

Reminding me that medicine was free in Italy and that Farnese's aging population had an inordinate amount of time on their hands, he told me of the social value of visits to the doctor. After all, the waiting room was pretty comfortable, especially during the summer hot spell, and it served as a place to catch up with friends and the local gossip. And when you got a little bored you could, like the doctor, go out and take a coffee.

He reaffirmed that the doctor was truly a good man, as well as a good doctor, and added that when the doctor is on vacation and people need to go to the doctor in the next town, nobody seems to get sick. So the question buzzing in our brains was: how many were here simply for the social aspect? After all, for much of the aging population in Farnese, there just was not that much to do on a summer morning.

MORE HEALTHCARE ITALIANO

Then there was the young "Doctor Kildare" who treated me at the clinic in Pitigliano. What better to break up the monotony of a day treating elderly Italians than a visitor from America, whose Italian wife left home to make a new life there? Maybe he too could go to America, marry, and make a new life. After all, he told Laura, he had seen how lovely American girls are on television. But for now, he would have to settle for treating the locals, filling out and stamping myriad government forms, and occasionally resting his healing hands on one of the adoring nurses. And I add that I took in all this while I lay on the gurney, waiting to be treated and feeling totally ignored.

ON ITALIAN TIME

In the beginning, I found it really difficult to adjust to the Italian sense of "get around to it." For so long I had managed time with a business person's sense of specificity: "Meeting Thursday, July 21, 8:30 to 9:15 in the Waterside conference room. Objective to finalize…" Now it was more along the lines of "we will meet tomorrow," with no specific time, followed by a series of phone calls or attempted phone calls to determine that the meeting will be either at six or perhaps seven.

"Do we have a reservation?" I would usually inquire, when the meeting involved lunch or dinner, often to hear a response like, "Yes, at eight thirty, but we don't have to be there then." I doubt there is a word in the Italian language for "precision."

I worked hard to hold it together, until one day early on when I was about to board a train. To confirm I was where I needed to be, I asked the conductor if the train would stop at Montalto di Castro, only to have him reply, "Maybe." From that point on, I realized if I wanted to maintain my sanity in Italy, I would simply have to go with the flow.

THE EPITOME OF INEFFICIENCY

It was not just the young doctor who looked admiringly at what he believed life in America to be like. More than a few people have complimented Laura for her wisdom to move to the land of opportunity, while expressing frustrations with Italy from a socioeconomic perspective.

One morning, our olive oil friend Domenico stopped by and went off on a rant about the Italian government, starting with the local school system. It seems they have to teach French rather than English because there are French teachers in the school, who are entitled to employment. Yes. English is the language of global commerce with an estimated one sixth of the world's inhabitants having at least a rudimentary understanding. It struck me that in socialistic Italy the government, with good intention, attempted to legislate employment without regard for market forces.

Domenico was really revved up, and the rant was gaining momentum as he paced and puffed on an uninterrupted chain of cigarettes. "And then there are the five janitors in the school. One to clean and four to watch. Anyway, why does Italy, with a population of 60 million, require more congressmen than America with over 300 million citizens?"

We understood his frustration, having gone countless times to the ATM only to find computers down, or the bank to find they had lost our records. There was also the hospital, where you had to go in person to make an appointment, only to be told to come back tomorrow because the computers were not working properly, and there was the hour it took to *almost* establish a mobile phone account. "Yes. Come back tomorrow to complete it," was the common rejoinder.

The bank in particular stood out as the absolute epitome of bureaucratic stultification. While technically it functioned as a bank, in reality it was Posta Italia, the Italian post office, for in Italy, as in other European countries, the post office provides, or in the case of Posta Italia *attempts* to provide, a multitude of different services. The services that the private sector provides reasonably well in the states did not seem to function well in Italy, where they are managed by a government that *itself* does not function well.

On first arriving, Laura established an account at the postal branch in Casal Palocco, Rome, the community where her sister lives. Being a fairly populous part of Rome, it was a very busy place. To do business there, you had to take a number, similar to a deli counter in an American grocery store. Since I had learned years ago from waiting to board ski lifts in the Italian Alps that forming and maintaining an orderly line runs contrary to Italian DNA, I could appreciate that the only way Posta Italia could avoid absolute bedlam was to install this numbering system.

Even the small post office in Farnese with a population of 1,602 uses the numbering system. I was taken aback when we first stepped into our town's forty square meter waiting room to find it chockablock with boisterous Farnesini. Some sat patiently, but others paced and grumbled. I soon found out it was not so much the wait that concerned them; they expected that. It was the nature of their visits, for it seemed that the regular clerk was out recuperating from surgery, and the replacement was having a difficult time delivering the mail to the proper recipients. It seemed everyone was getting someone else's mail and none of their own, and much of the town was in an uproar about it.

Early on in our adventure, we had to go back to the Casal Palocco branch to cancel our missing bank card and replace it with a new one. Evidently this had to be done in the branch that originated the card. We were prepared for this to be a fairly time-consuming process. No problem when we arrived to find standing room only in the anteroom and bunches of customers milling about in front of the building or shrugging their shoulders and heading off to the closest bar for a coffee. We drew number "e 84," and nonplussed, resigned ourselves to go with the flow. After all, weren't we in Italy?

Happily, the wait turned out to be well under an hour, and the time Laura spent at the window filling out myriad forms ran about the same length of time, so even for this guy, who was generally expecting things to be done in "a New York minute," it wasn't overly long or aggravating. The mind-numbing frustration set in when we returned from Farnese two weeks later, in anticipation that the new card would be available. We had accepted the policy that required us to return about a hundred miles to the office that had originated the account and were prepared to pick a number and wait our turn. Just go with the flow.

Fortune seemed to favor us as Laura's number came up in the marquee above the window of the same very pleasant associate who had serviced her last time. They both smiled in recognition of one another, and I told myself that we would be out of there in a jiffy and over to sister Adriana's for a splendid lunch. I must have forgotten that I was in Italy, for before I knew it, a rather chagrined associate was explaining to my highly annoyed spouse that there was no record of her application for a new card.

"Si," the woman remembered filing the application for Laura just a couple of weeks back, but inexplicably there was no record of the filing. Computers were checked. Manual file folders, the likes of the national archives, were searched. Supervisors were called over, but just no record anywhere. This being Italy, associates shrugged, myriad forms were once again filled out, and we resigned ourselves to losing another four hours of our lives driving to Rome and back in hopes that the process would finally work. We chalked it up to public sector waste. What can you do? Go to lunch. And in Italy that will surely cure your frustrations.

Eventually the card was replaced. Upon returning to the Casal Palocco branch of the post office, we saw a sign indicating it was being remodeled and that business usually handled there would be now handled at the neighboring town of Infernetto (an entire town that had been constructed without the builder having obtained permits, we learned). So off we went, another post office and another queue. Eventually and to my astonishment, the new card was delivered and we determined that in order to use as much of our remaining time on this planet pleasurably, we would sever our relationship with Posta Italia and close out the account. Laura told the clerk in business-like and polite terms that it was game over. The clerk responded in an equally polite and business-like manner that she would need to see the woman in the office at the other end of the building, who was responsible for closing out accounts. Not to be taken aback, Laura asked him to contact her so she could continue the transaction, but he replied that the woman saw people by appointment only. Chagrined, she asked how one went about making an appointment. Sympathetically the clerk responded that she would have to schedule the appointment with the woman herself and then, unprompted, volunteered that the woman was not in today. "Whose money is it, anyway," we grumbled most of the way back to Farnese.

SO MUCH TO SEE

Domenico reminded us that Italy, after all, is beautiful, and understanding that our relationship with La Signora was destined to be short-lived, he was determined to find us a house of our own in Farnese. And it truly is beautiful. Summer temperatures were in the mid and high eighties during the day. The farmers got an early start. We would hear tractors as early as five in the morning and then again as dusk approached. But between one and four things were quiet. The fields turned brown and the sheep were shorn. At the *borgo* we enjoyed a pretty constant breeze and found it pleasant to eat lunch under the awnings in the backyard.

I marveled at how unknown this patch of Italy in northern Lazio is to the outside world. This accounts for much of its genuine beauty. It is Italy pretty much untarnished. One of the attractions of the location that we highlighted in promoting the *borgo* was the relative proximity to Rome, Florence, Siena, Assisi and other guidebook must-sees. Those places are magnificent, but tourism has changed the essential nature of their surroundings. Visitors see, photograph and enjoy, but seldom feel and interact. However, we found so much in our immediate vicinity that there just was not time to venture further.

Northern Lazio, in our estimation, has as much to offer as Umbria or Tuscany. It is an overlooked gem. Its proximity to Rome and Leonardo da Vinci airport, in combination with the inflated prices of land and living expenses in Tuscany and Umbria, create the ideal scenario for future growth. How truly Italian are those regions anymore anyway? After all, don't my British friends refer to Tuscany as "Chianti-shire"? Our region offers more in that it remains so genuinely Italian. It has not been compromised by legions of tourists, seeking out tee-shirt shops and busily taking photographs of sights filled with other tourists. Several outings reinforced my conclusion.

NOT IN THE GUIDEBOOKS

One outing that showed the beauty and history of northern Lazio was a trip to an ancient necropolis, a cave known as a hermitage. Only available to the intrepid, those willing to hike for about forty-five minutes up and down hills along a riverbank and through a farmer's field, the cave is believed to go back to the twelfth century when it served as the home of hermits, who chose to lead their lives apart from society, in prayer and in harmony with nature.

With directions from Liam, Laura and I drove about twelve minutes to a point where we found a dirt road that descended several hundred yards to a river bank and a small flat area where we were able to park the Peugeot. We then worked our way around a wire fence and began to follow the river bank in the direction Liam had specified. It wasn't an easy hike since the trail along the bank was overgrown, and at the better part of an hour into the journey, I began to wonder if we had made a wrong turn or if, worse still, we were engaged in a wild goose chase. Then, sort of crashing through the undergrowth, we nearly stumbled into a clearing and an eye-popping view. We stood on flat rock, taking in the vision of a shallow pond filled with glistening water, fed from a narrow waterfall that seemed to bisect a massive cliff. I would guess it was between sixty and eighty feet high with a span of forty to fifty feet. Toward the top and off to one side sat the roughly five-foot opening to the cave. So the last fifty or sixty yards of the journey involved a steep climb along a narrow pathway. For me, it was a bit daunting and a cause for second thoughts. Once inside the dwelling it took a few seconds for the eyes to adjust to the dark before resting on an altar and an episcopal chair carved in stone. The walls contained paintings reflecting not only the ancient inhabitants' worship of God and his Blessed Mother, but also graphic symbols of male and female fertility. My imagination took me back in time. More so than when viewing some of Italy's most renowned and majestic ruins which were always surrounded by or even occupied by legions of tourists. At once I found myself having thoughts about the ancient church and the cryptography, symbols and codes featured in the novels of Dan Brown. We were one of a few fortunate enough to see a window into another world, unspoiled by the modern one.

Another outing took us to the ancient town of Castro, which ceased to be a town at some point in the sixteen hundreds. Castro, and the title of Duke of Castro, was gifted to the son of a powerful pope from the Farnese family, and with it possession of all the land from the Tyrrhenian Sea to Lake Bolsena. In an effort to further expand the family empire, the pope handed over additional lands to the north, as far away as Parma. Apparently, this land grab was viewed as going too far in the eyes of the Spanish, who occupied much of Italy at the time, and the duke was assassinated. The rival Barberini family eventually gained the power of the papacy, but still feared the Castros, so the Barberini pope gave a month's warning before sending a French army, one thousand strong, to raze the then magnificent city to the ground. Remnants of the power the Castros once wielded remain in the names of towns such as Grotte di Castro, Montalto di Castro and Ischia di Castro.

Over the years, vandals stole remains of the city and sold them on the black market (La Signora boasts that the marble on one staircase at the *borgo* came from Castro). In the 1990s some significant excavation took place. Today, after a short hike through the woods, one can see the remains of what was once the "shopping mall," complete with a hotel and functioning sewage system, the likes of which did not even exist in cities like Paris or London at the time. But thanks largely to mother nature and also a bit to the looters, all that remains are sections of columns and arches, piles of old Roman bricks and openings to the remains of now underground dwellings. At what was once the church of Saint Mary, only a single partial wall remains, with fragments of frescoes, and parts of the altar. A tribute to the fact that nothing—at least in this life—is forever.

The thing about visiting sights like the hermit's cave or the remains of the city of Castro is the experience of communion with the past, the timelessness. None of this is as easily achieved at more popular sites bubbling over with visitors barely removed from the surrounding twenty-first century.

SUMMER IS BEACH TIME IN ITALY

The Italian beach customs have always struck me as a bit odd, and for the most part unappealing. Italians like to cluster at the beach. The scene is row upon row, column upon column of lounge chairs, umbrellas, and beach towels, each hosting a pair of sunglasses and one or two slim pieces of swimsuit atop what might be the world's most fantastic collection of bronzed bods.

I preferred the lake, which is generally not crowded and where tall shade trees and fresh grass substitute for the hot Mediterranean sands. But one day we went with a group of locals to a beach just north of the Argentario, a part of the town of Albinia. We were told that the beach was attractive but not too commercial, therefore not overly crowded.

At a little before nine in the morning, I opened the gate, fired up the Peugeot and led our five-car caravan through the arch, then turned left into town where we caught up with our new local friends and started to head out of town. We hadn't gotten very far when Liam, now the lead driver, pulled over in front of a small apartment, and a smartly dressed young lady crossed the street and jumped in the car. Off we went toward the Tuscan border, up the mountain, through the town of Manciano, and down to the coast. In just over an hour's drive through magnificent countryside, we reached our objective. We drove into a pine grove and located parking places, unpacked the cars, and headed down a path through the brush. It was a short walk, and before we knew it we were in the sand and looking out at the blue Mediterranean Sea. Or perhaps it was the Tyrrhenian Sea. I am not sure at what point the Mediterranean becomes the Tyrrhenian and don't really understand how it can be both, which it seems to be. But one thing I am certain of is that it is awesome.

We wandered the fairly open stretch and soon staked out our territory with beach umbrellas. Next, we spread out towels and blankets and settled in. Before most of us could finish doffing sweatshirts or other beach cover ups, the kids were splashing in the surf. Having decided that there were enough English speakers in our assemblage who could help me out, I decided to chat up the Italian members of our party as best I could. Suddenly I was struck by the quiet beauty of the young lady who joined our party just before we pulled out of Farnese. I recognized her as the ever pleasant woman who worked behind the cheese counter at Giovanni's market, the one with the sweet, perpetual smile. She was stunning in her white beach togs and bronzed skin, with a cute tattoo on her shoulder. She caught Francis' eye, and I heard him announce to Michelle and Monica that never again would he shop at any market other than Giovanni's. We chatted for a bit, using Laura and Gabriella as interpreters. Later I commented on her beauty and sweetness to Liam. He told us she had become a dear friend and he would like to find her a nice Irish husband, as she never would consider any of the local chaps. He went on to say how she spent something like fourteen years cloistered in the local convent. I was stunned by this. I told Liam that she is much too lovely to be cloistered away in a convent. He agreed as I settled myself into one of the beach chairs. Then I began to wonder. Do all nuns have tattoos under those veils and habits?

AMICI, FRIENDS

When I reached into the car with the morning's groceries one day, I was a bit startled by a thumping sound. I turned to see two cantaloupe melons rolling into the back seat and then a beaming Giovanni, the grocer. No language barrier was going to deter him from expressing his gratitude and friendship. And that really was typical of how our neighbors in Farnese welcomed us and made us feel a part of the community.

Giovanni's is an interesting story. His father died when he was eleven, and he was forced to leave home and do farm work to support his mother and four sisters. But he found a way to go to school and now has what appears to be a solid family business, employing his sister and seventeen-year-old son. But Giovanni is only one friend and one story.

There was Amabile, who cooked for our guests and turned out some of the best pastries I could imagine. Her husband delivered firewood, and her daughter worked at Rokkabar. Domenico, who tended the olive groves, cleared our back field, supplied us with what he claimed to be the world's finest olive oil (I think he has got that right and I thought of working with him to export it to some specialty shops and high end restaurants in the states), delivered our wine, searched out real estate for us to buy, and gave me needles in the butt (more on that later).

Rosaria ran one of the most unique galleries I have ever seen, and then there were the sisters who ran the Rokkabar. They didn't seem to be able to speak in normal tones, but rather shout with glee as they sassed their regular customers.

Closer to us was the Polish couple, Maria and Josef, who helped take care of the *borgo*. Maria was stout and hearty, looking years older than her fifty-some years, a reflection of a hard life. Josef, in contrast to his fair-skinned wife, was tanned from work in the Italian sunshine. He looked rugged and portly at the same time. With an ever present cigarette dangling from his lips, his constant smile displayed the gaps where he once had teeth.

The hard-working couple came from southern Poland nine years earlier to help with the olive harvest and stayed on. Life in Italy beat the pants off the twenty-seven years Josef spent in the coal mines back in Poland. My communications with him were even more limited than with Italians, but a fist pump, hearty laugh and twinkle in his eye said a lot to me.

It disturbs me when in this day and age I see anyone in the process of self-destructing via the "evil weed" of smoking, but after twenty-seven years in a coal mine, I have to wonder what additional harm can be done.

Maria was a doll and a diligent worker. For Laura she was *simpatica*, that is understanding and sympathetic regarding the trials with La Signora.

We felt it an honor to be invited to their tiny apartment decorated with shrines to Mary and pictures of the late Polish pope John Paul, where we shared flavored vodka, kielbasa and chocolate. Josef displayed universal parental pride as he showed us a photo of his hulking son in the uniform of the provincial rugby team, just as back in Connecticut I proudly displayed photos of the kids involved in various sports. Maria could not feed us enough and insisted we take a bundle of kielbasa back to the *borgo* when we finally managed to break away.

I enjoyed talking to some of the teenagers who saw me as an opportunity to practice their English. One who worked as a waiter at Rokkabar struck me as especially fluent. I learned that his name was Kevin and inquired if perhaps one of his parents might be of Anglo origin, only to learn that they were not, and in fact were avowed communists and his brother was named Yuri. His hobby was ballroom dancing and he excelled at it along with his academics.

But closest of all were Liam and Gabriella. In a way they were our window to the Farnese world, and Liam wasn't even Italian. He had given up a career with IBM in Ireland to move his young family to Farnese, Gabriella's hometown. In Farnese he tended six hundred olive trees, shared his vineyard with family, worked virtually for an American pharmaceutical marketing research company, and found time to work on Farnese's town council while raising his three children. And with all that he still found time to lead me on some harrowing bike rides. His fourteen- and ten-year-old sons, Vincenzo and Enzo, buddied up with my fourteen-year-old and ten-year-old grandsons, Jake and Nick. Vincenzo and Enzo introduced my guys to the twice daily soccer matches, took them to a great Mediterranean beach, taught them a few words in Italian and got Nick speaking his mother tongue with an Irish brogue.

One night Liam and Gabriella hosted a dinner for twenty-three with enough food and drink for seventy-three. I doubt Hollywood could have staged a more classic Italian setting with a villa nestled on a hilltop amidst the vineyards and olive groves. Gabriella loved to cook, and the kitchen, which she designed herself, was larger than the entire square footage of most Italian homes. Amid vibrant conversation in a mixture of English, Italian, and pantomime, we devoured course after course late into the night, each one better than the preceding. I am too embarrassed to recap the amount of Prosecco, Spumante red wine, white wine, beer and sangria that accompanied the meal. Okay. We drank some mineral water as well. Sitting in the middle of the long table opposite Liam, I picked up smidgeons of conversation up and down the table. Most were interspersed with laughter. After a while, it struck me as curious that bouts of loud laughter continuously emanated from the end of the table where my daughter and son sat opposite two rather refined looking women. At a point when we got up and ventured to the table with an abundant display of dolci, I encountered Monica and inquired as to what could possibly be so funny. "Your son," she replied with a wide grin. "It is his limited Italian. It seems that if he cannot remember the correct response in Italian, he responds to their questions in proper Italian, but he is simply making up the answers to suit what he can manage to say in Italian. He is being very polite and the ladies are properly pleased although terribly misled."

Monica then went on to describe how Francis (who always introduces himself as "Francesco" when speaking to Italians) explained to the ladies that he lived on the Monterey Peninsula in California only to receive the gleeful response that they knew of the area as the home of the well-known actor and director, Clint Eastwood. And did Fran happen to know him? Apparently anxious to continue the conversation, the fabrication began with a description of the golf game the two had recently enjoyed together. Since the ladies were duly impressed, they followed with more questions which led to more fabrications….and a good time for all.

Back at the table, Liam whose olive orchard ended with a large satellite dish, began to pepper us with questions regarding recent programs he had viewed on Fox News.

Walking back to the borgo, I reflected on such a magical evening but also on how small the world was becoming.

ROOM FOR THE ENTIRE FAMILY

My sisters and their husbands visited us early on and our six grandkids all spent at least two weeks with us, as did their parents.

Our family and friends from New York and California took in Etruscan ruins, hiked and biked in the forest preserve, and made side trips to Rome, Florence, Siena and Orvieto. In between they swam in the lake, the Med, the river, a spa, a natural hot springs and a pool. Jake found a great swimming spot at the Med. At the end of the main drag in Porto Santo Stefano, and up a short hill past a number of hotels, is a narrow strip of land no more than fifteen feet in width and a hundred and fifty feet in length. We found parking on what appeared to be an abandoned helipad, and young and old made their way down the rocks to our special beach. The grandkids discovered a concrete structure poking about fifteen feet above the water surface. A knotted rope provided a means to climb to the top, from which they took plunge after plunge into the refreshing sea water.

Each adventurous day was followed by dinner, for as many as eighteen, under the back pergola or at a local trattoria.

Just hanging at the borgo turned out to be such a great source of joy. We sometimes wandered in the olive groves or checked the fruit trees for peaches, apricots, pears, figs and grapes. Or as the day dwindled down, we grabbed a carafe of wine and a few glasses and headed to the rooftop terrazzo. From there the views were both soft and spectacular. To the west we could often make out the sea in the distance, while turning north toward Tuscany the distant view took in Monte Amiata, the highest peak in southern Tuscany. To the east and south we saw checkerboard hills dotted with sheep and the occasional farmhouse or the red rooftops of Farnese. Looking closer to home, we observed the local cemetery. It was a garden of exquisite monuments. We joked about the quietness of our closest neighbors and marveled that the Italians really can do things efficiently when they choose to, because adjacent to the cemetery was the home for Farnese's elderly.

MORE FUN WITH THE ITALIAN HEALTH CARE SYSTEM

Another misadventure with health care turned out to be more comedy than anything. I had come down with an infection. Something about living on this side of the Atlantic, or perhaps my advanced age, was causing my pipes to rust. So we booked an appointment with a specialist who provided an hour and twenty minute anatomy lecture, complete with dirty pictures, and prescribed a number of medications, all of which could be obtained at the local pharmacy. Trying to understand the doctor called to my mind a movie scene in which Robert De Niro played a mad shrink. But this bedraggled looking doc seemed to know his stuff, and he reassured us that I was not in any imminent danger. So all smiles, we went off to the local *farmacia* with prescriptions in hand. After waiting our turn, all was going well until the pharmacist explained that the prescriptions called for injections to be administered twice a day. The process would be fairly tricky and we would need to have a doctor or nurse do it. As Laura explained our dilemma, not knowing if either would be available, a booming voice from the door of the pharmacy volunteered the Italian equivalent of "I'll do it."

I turned to see who else but Domenico, our tractor driver, olive grower, factotum. There was all 275 pounds of him, smiling from shoulder to shoulder (he seemingly has no neck). He always reminded me of a mature version of the Italian American kids from North Jersey, who regularly beat my butt on the American football fields a long time ago. I began to sweat.

However, Domenico's presence turned out to be a stroke of luck. He knew his stuff, having driven an ambulance at one stage in his career. Several days, half dozen shots in the butt, and I was as good as new. No sweat. Just a bit of discomfort sitting down. The kids and grandkids visiting at the time would all flash big grins or suppress giggles whenever Domenico would show up at the *borgo* and accompany me into one of the bedrooms, or when I would wince sitting down at the dinner table.

GETTING BETTER ACQUAINTED

As we became better acquainted with the town and its residents, we found ourselves drawn into the local politics. I got my education from Liam, who was a councilman and who was somewhat frustrated by the local situation. Liam brought an affable charm and that sense of politics that Irish Americans are noted for in the states. He topped all candidates in the last election, but because he was not an Italian citizen, he could not be the mayor. Instead, as a councilman he was responsible, among other things, for keeping the town clean. And it was an incredibly clean town. To make and keep it that way, Liam must drive down from his farmhouse in the hillside above town and rally the street cleaners each morning. As government employees who are unionized, they must be handled with kid gloves. Armed with bamboo brooms and clad in bright orange "armor," they can choose between attacking the streets or wandering off to a coffee and card game in one of the town's bars. Union strength prevents much from being done about someone who chooses the latter, so Liam has to motivate them to choose the former. The residents of Farnese take great pride in their town and expect it to be kept spanking clean; however, they view it as the government's job, not theirs. So if someone finds a bit of litter on the sidewalk, they call Liam rather than stoop to pick it up. As Liam explains it, the town has 1,604 residents, so as councilman he has 1,603 bosses. He told us how the town is pretty much divided between members of his party and the opposing communist party, and that the administration often swings back and forth each election cycle.

We of course gravitated to the party in power. Perhaps it was because of our friendship with Liam, or my conservative leanings, or Laura's very staunch positions on the right. I suspect that in some way they were all connected to finding ourselves invited to a dinner for the administration and some top supporters.

I was thrilled at the invitation and conjured up images of pasta platters, beef from free range cows, and piles of fresh vegetables. Perhaps, if I was lucky, there would be some zucchini flowers stuffed with mozzarella cheese and a dash of sardines, followed by assorted cheeses and a *dolce*. Of course, all of this would be following a bubbly prosecco toast and washed down with liters of *vino locale*.

Laura, too, was thrilled at the invitation, but for different reasons. This would be a chance to set the mayor straight on what Farnese needed to do to further improve its appearance. We had heard that the town's chief executive was a legitimate double dipper. He was paid a full salary from the *provincia* (the region), but was given two days a week to perform his duties to Farnese as mayor. And for that he was paid an additional salary from the *Comune* (the town hall). We were not sure if either body knew which one he was working for on any given day, and wondered further if he was actually working for either. Laura had a list already assembled and on the tip of her tongue: neglected empty planters in front of the school, a broken net on the tennis court, and the torn up carpet on the kids' "football" field.

The dinner came off as anticipated. The evening was lovely with an inviting breeze, and sumptuous food and wines were in abundance. Laura managed to sit next to the mayor and had his ear throughout the meal. She found him a bit defensive, but as he enjoyed the food and drink, he seemed to become more accommodating, ultimately thanking her and assuring her that her concerns would be met.

And of course, nothing ever came of it.

COPING WITH THE LANGUAGE

Some people have an ear for language. But not all people and certainly not this person. Somehow, I completed my language requirements at school, but managed to do so without learning even a smattering of the French I was studying. Laura, by contrast, has the ear and the brain for language. She came to the states from Italy to attend Barry College without ever having studied English and graduated Magna Cum Laude three and a half years later speaking fluent English with just the faintest but charming hint of an accent. After graduation she wanted to remain in the states, and that meant acquiring a job and a green card. When she looked around for available work opportunities, she located a school in North Jersey, not too far from the Big Apple, that was looking for a language teacher. Not Italian or French, her second language, but Spanish. No problem for her; she had taken courses at school along with some Russian.

Our three children take after her. All three manage well in Italian and have demonstrated competency in other languages. My excuse was never having been exposed to a second language in an authentic environment. The time in Italy was supposed to change all that, but it did not seem to happen. After all I had my crutch—my wife—and in fairness the language spoken at the *borgo* was usually English. But when going to the market or going out by myself, I was forced to attempt my pidgin Italian to the dismay or amusement of whomever had the misfortune of listening.

They say that a little bit of knowledge is a dangerous thing, and I have found that to be especially true concerning languages. How often have I just picked up a few words out of a conversation and come away with a totally wrong impression? Like the day when a couple of lovely but especially rotund friends said they would join us at the lake "*senza costume*," which I correctly understood to mean without swimsuits. Italian women do have a different sense of modesty than their American counterparts, much to the delight of Italian men and probably to the chagrin of fabric manufacturers. However, overhearing the women's plans conjured up a rather unpleasant vision of skinny dipping. As liberated and flexible as I want to see myself, there was no way I wanted to be associated with this situation. As soon as they were out of earshot, I pulled Laura aside and expressed my concern that such behavior would be, well, inappropriate, as I explained what I had understood. Bursting into laughter, she shook her head in dismay and explained that *senza costume* simply meant they would not bring their swim togs because they did not plan to swim.

It was not just the spoken word that gave me trouble, as I was pretty good at misinterpreting the written word as well. For example, there was the day I took the car to the car wash, walked up to the coin box, thrust my six euros into the slot. Out dropped a package of prophylactics. If I had read the instructions properly, I would have realized that the people who installed the coin operated carwash had also set up a little coin operated side business. I wasted six euros as I dropped my unwanted purchase to the ground like a package of hot coals. What would people think of a seventy-year-old bounding about with a pack of rubbers? Laura reminded me that this was indeed Italy, and people might think I was just another politician. Then I began to wonder if anyone associated a shiny clean vehicle as a sex magnet.

I was determined that being language challenged would not deter me. On one exceptionally delightful day, I decided to bike along the shores of Lake Bolsena. I was pedaling happily along, feeling all was right with the universe, when I came across three seniors struggling to launch a *gommone*, an inflatable boat with an outboard motor. I hopped off my bike and inquired "*Aiuto?*" Do you need help?

The man responded "*Sì*" and motioned to push from one side, instructing in his own limited Italian. I responded, bumbling out some suggestions as to how we might go about our mission. He slowly concurred, and I put my shoulder to the stern. As I pushed, I found myself reverting to English: "One, two, three." The boat slid easily into the water, and the owner turned to me with a smile and announced in flawless English: "Thank you so much. That was absolutely brilliant."

The four of us doubled over with laughter.

Going to the market presented an opportunity to really test my Italian. One day I was assigned to pick up the necessary groceries for the meal Amabile and Laura were planning for our artist visitors. I carefully noted each item on my iPhone, and after putting the kitchen back in order from breakfast, set off to Giovanni's market. Upon entering, I offered Assunta a bright *"Buongiorno."* From behind the counter she smiled, and in a manner that might be reserved for someone who had just successfully published a doctoral dissertation, offered *"Bravo,* Terry."

We were actually engaged in a dialogue in Italian. Brimming with confidence, I pulled my iPhone from my pocket and started to read the grocery list. *"Prosciutto,"* I hummed out.

"Si," she replied, and quickly produced a packet of the cured uncooked thin-sliced ham.

"Due formaggi (two cheeses)," I countered, my confidence swelling.

"Si, romano," Assunta responded, producing some already packaged Pecorino Romano cheese. *"Ed un pezzetto di parmigiano,"* she added, producing a package of the other Italian culinary staple. Then a third item: *"Ecco il tuo salame* (here's your salami)."

I am sure a puzzled look flashed across my face. Was she telepathic? Sensing my puzzlement, Assunta explained that Amabile had stopped by and told her that Terry would be coming by to order the following items.

Anyhow, being language challenged isn't all bad, as I discovered one day when Laura and I were invited to an all-day "eat-a-thon" with some local shepherds and their families. We sat at a makeshift table constructed for the event from old planks sitting on top of concrete blocks and stacks of old tires. The table stretched from one end of the long barn to the other, seating at least fifty of us. All but a very few were related.

It took a fair amount of time to meet, shake hands, and exchange remarks, most of which I could not completely understand, with the various aunts, uncles, nieces, nephews, cousins and spouses. It seemed that so and so's cousin was also so and so's mother and the sister-in-law of… Fortunately for me, the Italian word "nipoti" covers nieces, nephews, grandchildren and other relatives.

As the meal progressed and the wine was poured, the conversation became more animated, and it became obvious that I was floundering in my attempts to participate in the conversation. As the women passed up and down the makeshift table dishing out pasta, bread, roasted beef, roasted lamb, and roasted pork, they noted my silence, and just as they would with an infant who hadn't yet developed speech, they insisted upon feeding me, piling extra helping after extra helping onto my plate. It didn't stop with the entrees. It seemed that most of the fine ladies had prepared their special dessert recipe, and the men had brought their very best wines. It would not have been polite to refuse, especially since my limited language would not have let me do so discreetly. So like a child, I simply ate and drank and left the solving of the world's problems to others.

L'ACCIDENTE, THE ACCIDENT

We had visits from my niece and nephew and their spouses and decided to treat them to a hike to the hermitage, the likes of which they would never see in their hometowns in North Carolina and Texas. After exploring the waterfall, cave and its paintings, we hiked back to the road. Noticing that it was getting late, I decided to return via a shortcut over an unpaved road, what the locals called a white road. We mounted up in three vehicles, and upon my son-in-law Pete's wagon train command to "move 'em out," I led our three car caravan rather slowly down the road looking for the turn off. Before long, our trail was intercepted by a shepherd and his flock. Our caravan came to a complete stop and remained that way for a number of minutes until the last little lamb passed by. I had no sooner thrust the shift lever into gear when I caught sight of the turn off. Flipping the directional, I gave a hand signal to the wagoneers behind me and began to change lanes. At the same time, I heard a loud squealing of brakes and in the rearview mirror saw the car behind hurtling toward us. Life went into slow motion. I felt a jarring crash and wondered what Pete was trying to do. How could he be going so fast, and how could he hit us so hard?

"Are you okay? Hurt? Anyone?" I was bellowing. All assured and reassured me they were fine, so I unbuckled and bolted from the car, instantly realizing that the large gray projectile that pancaked the back of my trusty Peugeot was not Pete's car but a small Mercedes wagon, carrying no fewer than six screaming Italians.

I only recognized a couple of words. They were not nice words, and they were directed at me. I told them they were wasting their breath and attempted to inquire if anyone was hurt. They looked okay to me, and if the rising decibel level was any indicator, they surely sounded unhurt. I asked my daughter Monica to serve as a translator, and she attempted to calm them down, explaining that I did not have a command of their mother tongue, but spoke English. I recognized that they began to rant in a rude and uncomplimentary manner about the English. Monica eventually got it across to them that we were American and that we must exchange details. They stopped bashing the Brits but continued to yell and glare.

"Seems they don't like Americans either," she translated for me.

"Too bad," I replied. I told myself that I was not at fault, since they had somehow sped out from nowhere, passed two cars and rear-ended me. Regardless, I had insurance without a deductible. And most importantly, no one appeared to be injured. I asked Pete to see if my car could be moved off the road. As he got in and started it up, there was another uproar. I tried to explain that he was simply pulling it over in order that it not attract a second collision. Finally, they got the idea and calmed down a tad. They continued trying to ignore Monica to take their wrath out on me. I began to wonder if they were related to La Signora or if she had put them up to it.

Monica explained to me that they wanted to fill out the accident report indicating that I cut in front of them, failing to provide any signal. I told Monica that they should fill out the report, and I would add my proper understanding of the event and sign off under my remarks. Monica patiently explained, dealing with numerous interruptions. Thinking we were in the process of putting the matter to bed, I suggested to Pete that he and the cousins continue toward home. As I turned back to my antagonists, I saw that the three men had stepped back into the field and were motioning me to join them. One in particular appeared to be especially menacing, with a haircut about the height and style universally popular in a Marine Corps boot camp and bulging biceps with what suggested twofer days at the tattoo parlor. Quickly I told Pete not to leave but instead to get Jeff and Tim and join me in the field. Both Pete and Jeff stand well over six foot and Tim, while smaller, still carries the look of the Texas footballer he was in high school. Suddenly there were conciliatory gestures and moderate tones. I was relieved and Monica and one of the women started exchanging details and turning to the accident report form. But then a new problem arose. The report forms, which came with the Peugeot, were in French and English. Monica could handle either one, but no one from the other party could handle anything other than Italian. Just when the guys started getting testy once again, along came the *carabinieri*, the Italian police. The decibel level rose higher, and I discerned that the Italian guys surmised that we called them behind their backs. Monica told them that we did not and eventually the presence of the *carabinieri* had a calming effect. With some reluctance, one officer got out of the car. I asked if he spoke English, and he immediately shook his head and looked toward Monica, who was holding the French/English accident report form. I noticed a look of relief on his face until Monica explained that we had encountered another language issue. He then went to his car and rummaged around for an Italian version of the form, but without success. Then Tim's wife Jen saved the day by producing the forms in Italian she found in the car she had rented at the Rome airport. I began to wonder if the Italian car rental agencies simply expected drivers to have accidents.

Next followed a discussion of the location of the accident. The road sign at the intersection referred to the "Trail of the Briganti," but the officer correctly pointed out that nearly every white road from here to Bolsena is designated "Trail of the Briganti." He shrugged and got back in the car, rejoining his partner who had never bothered to get out of the car. They quickly drove off as if nothing out of the ordinary had happened, and I realized their true concern was that they not be late for dinner.

And so, the forms got filled out, and I was asked to sign off. Through Monica, I advised them of my correction, which was immediately followed by another eruption. Monica explained that if I signed, the insurance companies would settle. Otherwise there might be a court action. I asked her to translate, "No way would I sign something which was not true. How could I not signal when I had two cars following me and looking for my directions to find the way? How anxious and impatient to get back to Rome was the other party that they had to pass two cars at breakneck speed and with a child not sitting in a car seat but on a passenger's lap? And what could they have been drinking for lunch?"

After nearly two hours we did prevail. I felt concerned for them, especially for the children, so we offered to help by driving them to the Montalto train station. When the excitement had subsided, I began to feel drained. Wishing them the best of luck, I got back into what was now only four fifths of a Peugeot 508 and headed for the *borgo*, knowing I would need to explain to Laura the reason we were late for dinner.

As I passed through the gate and under the arch to the back of the *casale*, she came into view. A little closer and there was no way to miss the stern look she shot toward us. And then it quickly transformed to one of total incredulousness as she took in what had once been the rear portions of the vehicle. For appearance's sake, I backed the car into its usual spot, opened the door, and offered to explain.

"Maybe you should have a glass of wine first," she volunteered, sympathetically.

To my relief, Peugeot came through with excellent customer service. By noontime the next day, they had replaced the wounded 508 with another. It was the same color and had an extra gear, six speeds instead of five. And in the short interim, not one but three Italian friends had offered to loan us their car.

THE SERPENTE, THE SNAKE

Google the Lamone, the huge national forest preserve that borders on Farnese. Before long you will read about the *cinghiali*, the wild boar, and the *vipere*. The viper is known to be deadly venomous and can be quick to strike if taken unaware. (Some historians tell us it was a *vipera* and not Marcus Antonius who did in Cleopatra). The thought of encountering a *vipera* on one of our hikes left an impression on us both, but more so on Laura, who grew up as a city girl. Her unease was dramatically reinforced by a conversation with one of our neighbors, who told her never to go into the Lamone from May until October, for fear of the deadly reptiles. May until October! That just happened to be the extent of our stay. But as it turned out, I hiked and biked throughout that reserve without ever encountering the dangerous creatures. I had pretty much forgotten about them until one otherwise uneventful day, when Laura and I and the visiting cousins returned from a day at the sea. She noticed that one of the branches in the wood pile was wiggling around. Immediately and correctly, she concluded it was a snake and quite possibly a *vipera*.

Needless to say, she was anything but pleased with her discovery, which she loudly called to my attention, somehow giving the impression that I was responsible for it being there. When I did not share her alarm but rather cautiously avoided the wood pile, while trying to determine the best course of action, she quickly concluded that I would be no match for the snake and started rattling off names of people she had better call to properly deal with the intruder. A pleasant couple, Rosa and Rosario, cared for a nearby farm, and Rosario drew the short straw.

In the meantime, my nephew Tim and my niece's husband Jeff sized up the creature from what they believed to be a safe distance, while niece Megan mumbled something about preparing for a nervous breakdown before running into the house to stand on the couch. Tim, who grew up as an eagle scout in Texas, declared that the head was indeed diamond shaped, an indication that the creature was poisonous. The cats, who obviously had not been any help when the creature decided to slither across the patio and nestle in the wood pile, did nothing but stare at the creature.

Rosario arrived and took a calm approach, saying that the unwelcome visitor was larger than the typical *vipera*, but the head did appear to be sort of diamond shaped. Conventional wisdom mandated that we destroy the creature. But how?

"*Prendi un bastone*," Rosario declared. That uncomprehending look that I so often saw when I attempted to speak to people in Italian appeared on the cousins' faces until one confirmed in a puzzled tone that yes, certainly it was a bastard. I realized we were encountering a language issue, so I found myself attempting to translate.

"A *bastone* is a stick. Get a stick," I commanded, and cautiously approached the critter with grandson Nick's hiking stick.

"*Troppo piccolo*," Rosario told me as he approached with an eight or nine foot section of fence rail. He meant the stick was too small.

Fearing that the guys would tear apart the fence, I rushed into the house and retrieved two six foot long pizza paddles that were standing by the fireplace.

Rosario broke open the woodpile and pinned the creature down with the fence pole. As the creature wiggled frantically, Rosario abandoned his calm demeanor and shouted, "*spingere*" and "*la testa*" over and over while the cousins flailed around with their pizza paddles. Finally I realized that they had no idea what he was saying and translated: "The head, crush the head."

With no little effort, they crushed the snake's head as it twitched and twitched. Finally it gave up the ghost. Laura relaxed and Megan looked forward to maintaining her sanity. Relieved, I went into the house and fetched some cold beers. As the cousins recounted their own acts of bravery and toasted Rosario's leadership, he took out his *telefonino* and called an uncle, who he said would be able to provide positive identification. Of course by now, little remained of the late creature's cranium. Someone stretched the body out. It measured a good six feet. Tim said that in Texas it would make several belts or quite a few hat bands, and we busied ourselves snapping and sending photos off with our smartphones.

Mission accomplished, Rosario returned to his farming, and I had started about some chores when a car drove in. It was Rosario's uncle and an official from the forestry department. We had met the official before and witnessed that his manner suggested his importance, at least in his own mind.

He carefully examined the remains of the creature and proclaimed that it was not a *vipera* at all but a variety of snake that had the habit of drinking up any milk that might slip between a cow's udders and a calf's mouth.

"How cute," I muttered. Not an English speaker, he mistook my sarcasm for interest and mounted a virtual soapbox.

"Indeed, it was a vital element in the food chain which should be added to the endangered species list," Laura translated for us. We began to feel sorry that we did not know this an hour ago, but after all it was a snake.

Laura, who can love all things great and small, was now sympathetic and felt for the seemingly innocent and obviously unfortunate creature. She expressed her pity and shot me a look that I recognized. It's a look that told me I am a heartless, uncaring sort who should be ashamed of myself for taking such an innocent life.

But I couldn't manage to dredge up any remorse. Better safe than sorry. And had the pompous official really called it correctly? Rosario stopped back with a burlap to collect the remains, and then Liam stopped by. Both, along with the cousins, agreed that we had taken the most prudent action, and even if not venomous, the constrictor could have done serious harm, especially to children.

In the next few days, as life and feelings were returning to normal, we found ourselves face to face with another unwelcome visitor. It was the largest fox I had ever seen and as bold as any. This visitor showed no real fear, just a little concern for one little cat, who by now had adopted us and learned to behave. The fox froze and glared at the cat. The cat stared back at the fox for what seemed like minutes. Eventually the fox sauntered off, head hanging low. The little cat had stared him down.

A DEAR OLD FRIEND

In Farnese there is a process for getting fresh drinking water from the town. A machine dispenses water one liter at a time in user provided containers, at no cost for plain water and € .05 per liter for *frizzante*, or water with gas. There is a limit of nine liters at a time.

The machine was installed in order to meet an EU mandate regarding the quality of drinking water. Water from the tap did not meet the standards. Old timers snarled at the mandate, pointing out that they have become just that—old timers—in spite of having drunk town water for the better part of a century. Shopkeepers like Giovanni are even less thrilled, as the government's beneficence eats into their bottled water sales. Often there is a line in front of the machine, and as a result the process can be time consuming, which accounts for some additional grumping and insistence that out of towners are coming in and taking advantage of the EU's gift to Farnese. But since most people in Farnese have an overabundance of time, the water run can be a social occasion, not unlike the office gathering at the water cooler. This social aspect can be a mild annoyance to that small minority of us who did try to maintain some sense of a schedule.

My grandson, Nicholas, and I had become quite adept at filling our allotted nine liters rather quickly, but one Sunday the task fell to the less experienced Laura. I pulled into the parking area and chased her out of the car with nine empty plastic bottles, imploring her to quickly jump in line before too many Farneseans arrived looking to leisurely pass the time of day, while I maneuvered the car into the remaining tight parking spot.

As Laura waited in what somewhat resembled a line, she appeared to be happily engaged in the local chatter. Time started to drag, and I began to wonder what conversation could possibly be so interesting that filling just nine liters of water was taking so long. From where I sat in the car, I couldn't hear the conversation, but I wouldn't have understood much of it anyway. Looking to see if Laura needed help, I noticed the young man she was talking with adjusting his shorts to display a recent scar on his hip. Puzzling.

When Laura eventually returned to the car she was bubbling with excitement. She told me that the young man was from Ischia di Castro, the neighboring town, and that in the course of conversation Laura mentioned that her best friend from school, Aida, was a boarding student who came from Ischia to attend their private school in Rome. Laura had always wondered what had become of her and mentioned the family name. To this, the young man replied that the family was still very much a part of Ischia, and in fact it was Aida's brother, a surgeon, who had recently operated on his hip. That was the point at which he felt compelled to show off the scar. As proof, I guessed.

And of course he knew Aida, who had retired from teaching in the local school system, become a widow, and who like Laura herself had maintained her girlish figure. Laura was thrilled. Who would have thought that her very best school chum from Rome would have returned to this small town in the Tuscia region, married there, and lived on as a local school teacher? That sort of thing rarely happened in the states where we often move about whenever the opportunity presents itself, and it certainly had not happened in Laura's life.

The next day while we waited for dinner at the pizza parlor, Laura took her iPhone and began to google various spellings of the family name. She hit the target and hesitantly placed a call. Her face reflected nervous anticipation.

"*Pronto*, is this Aida? Did you go to school in Rome? Do you remember a Marialaura Ferrini?" I watched her face brighten and light up in as big a smile as I have ever seen. The response from the other end of the phone was obviously positive.

The adventurous young lady who had vanished to America over a half century before had just reconnected with her best childhood friend. She chatted, smiled, exchanged phone numbers and promised to meet soon. I could not have been more excited and thrilled for her.

The very next day Aida called, and arrangements were made for that afternoon. I took the phone and gave directions in English to her brother, who had moved to the states and happened to be visiting from Texas. To be certain they could find us, Aida asked through her brother if we knew anyone in town she could call if she got lost on the way. I immediately thought of Antonio, who had, like Aida, taught locally, while serving as the *sindaco* or mayor of Farnese, and whose daughter Maria was coming to visit with us later in the afternoon.

"Of course! Antonio was a dear friend," I heard her say in the background. I knew she had to wonder how her best friend, who had so quietly vanished to America, now happened to be in Farnese of all places, and in turn, was a friend of her friend, who was still considered by many to be the most important citizen of Farnese.

The next afternoon she came to the *borgo* with her brother. I met a very distinguished looking, lovely, and truly elegant lady and immediately understood the friendship. Her brother, now an Italian American, and I spoke of his family's origins, his home in San Antonio, Texas, and our life in the Northeast, while the former school chums spoke of the old days and other girls from their "*gruppo*." Aida had called one to tell her that she could never imagine who, after vanishing fifty years ago, had suddenly popped up in the neighboring town and whom she was about to visit. All afternoon their conversation bubbled. They discussed children and grandchildren, recounting a common part of their lives that they had spent together and a very uncommon part spent in very different manners. They had once been so connected and then so disconnected.

I thought of the sage advice of the famous Italian American, Yogi Berra: "When you get to the fork in the road, take it." They did, and it led in very different directions. Laura ventured to Florida, earned degrees from American universities, moved to New Jersey, and married an American who didn't have an iota of Italian DNA. Then she moved with him to Connecticut where they had several different homes, a ski home in Vermont, and a timeshare in Manhattan. She taught in American high schools, dabbled in her own food preparation business, computer programming, and finally a very satisfying career as a garden designer.

Aida, in contrast, had returned to her small town in Tuscia, taught in the local school system for 34 years, and married a local magistrate. They lived in the *palazzo* her father, a local banker, had built many years ago. She never traveled far, and had never even boarded an airplane nor sent an e-mail. Now retired, she sings in the local church choir at Saint Rocco's.

And now for a joyous time, their paths have merged as they walk arm and arm about the grounds of the *borgo*, discovering new things in common, such as that they are both very much in love with blond-haired granddaughters aged eight and nine named Caroline and Carolina.

AUGUST

In August, Farnese underwent a complete transformation. It was no longer the quiet little village we moved into back in May, because Farnese, like the rest of Italy, had changed. The change is known as *Ferragosto*. In mid-August, businesses hibernate and cities like Rome and Milan morph into ghost towns. Nearly everyone is on holiday. It is imbued into the national DNA, and even in times of financial crisis, it would be unthinkable for any self-respecting Italian to not go on holiday. The government, in its wisdom, recognizes the conflict between the citizen's duty to vacation and their economic constraints and comes forward with a special subsidy for those who need help supporting their vacation plans. After all, what is the matter with a little more red ink when national debt already exceeds GDP by over a quarter anyway? And perhaps there is some merit in the move, since such a significant chunk of the Italian economy depends on tourism. Anyhow, we heard it said that, for Italians, GDH is more important than GDP: Gross Domestic Happiness.

So Farnese and the Tuscia region seemed to be getting their share of visitors at this holiday time. Clearly the population had swollen. We measured the population increase by counting the tables in the *piazza* outside of Rokkabar. It contained six outdoor tables when we arrived in May. In July another dozen or so were added to one corner of the *piazza*. In August, dozens of tables covered nearly the entire *piazza*. And some nights, when we arrived for a late evening *limoncello* or brandy, we could hardly find a place to sit down.

Business at the *borgo* was good. We were getting several requests a day from Italian holiday planners seeking lodgings, but almost only for the weeks of *Ferragosto*. I told Laura that if only every week of the year could be moved into mid-August, our little business would gross a couple of hundred thousand euros per year. It seemed we were spending an hour or so each morning figuring and refiguring which parties could occupy which rooms, and then responding to inquiries.

"Three families want to stay for five days while their children attend music camp, but they don't feel they should pay for all five nights."

"Marco Romeo, an archeologist, came by to see if we could house some visiting professors, who are coming down from the north to visit the Bronze Age dig."

"If we move the family who are biking down from Siena to the apartments and free up the two rooms off the upstairs parlor…"

In spite of the road blocks thrown up by La Signora, we seemed to be making a success of running the *borgo*. Not that it was hard to improve, given the way things had been mismanaged in the past. But in addition to making the place livable, we had gotten a handle on the region's attractions and a pretty good sense of what people enjoyed most. The locals found good accommodations and seemed to find us acceptable, if not interesting hosts, given that we were Americans. The visitors from the states, especially the painters, reveled in the scenery and relished the food and drink. They appreciated the chance to experience Italy the way Italians do. I think a letter from Mary Frances Allen, a visitor from the San Francisco Bay Area, summed it up better than I can:

"Terry and Laura,
Thank you for your generosity and kindness in hosting us in Farnese. Thank you so much for meeting us at the train in Montalto di Castro. It was a very enjoyable evening listening to the band performance in the town square that evening. Thank you for taking me to Mass on Sunday and for the cappuccinos before and after — very memorable. I loved the Feast of the Assumption devotional procession through the inner and outer city at night with the chanting of the rosary. Then there was a nice hour-long walk along Lake Bolsena in the morning. The hike to the hermit cave was well worth the effort and the herd of sheep surrounding the car is one of my favorite memories. The Farnese Renaissance re-enactment pageant with the horses, costumes and flag ceremonies was spectacular. We stayed until they finished, close to midnight. The visit to Bagnoregio was breathtaking -- I may frame my photos or postcard. Our car tour to Porto Santo Stefano is memorable with the wonderful waterfront lunch and the crowd jumping off of the ruins into the sea. The dinner at the Taverna with the wild boar and artisan cooking was delicious. It was such a pleasant surprise finding an up to the minute establishment in the oldest part of the town. And, such a grand finale, with twenty-two people at a great dinner and barbecue, seeming so effortless. Thank you for housing us in such a nice place.

It was great to meet you and thank you, again, for such a memorable week.

With best wishes,
Mary Frances Allen

THE BISHOP VISITS FARNESE

The weather continued to be splendid as Laura returned from the market and announced that we had been invited to meet the bishop, who would be in town in a couple of days.

Okay.

I doubted that the bishop and I would have much to say to one another, but I learned that the invitation came from the nuns at the convent in town by way of Assunta, who as I have noted was once a member of their merry band. We felt compelled to accept, and in fact looked forward to a reception in the magnificent convent gardens that are normally not available for public viewing.

The occasion was the ceremony where one of the sisters takes her final vows. I had mixed feelings about lending my presence and with it my support to such an occasion. We had attended Sunday Mass in the beautiful chapel of the convent, and thanks to the splendor of the chapel and the music of the nuns, it had been a truly delightful and memorable experience. But I have this thing about young women abandoning their womanhood and closeting themselves away behind veils. In spite of the goodness I attribute to the nuns who taught me in my formative years, I tend to equate the nun's habit with the Islamic extremist's burka. But appreciating these fine ladies, respecting their tradition, and the fact that the invitations were delivered by our friend Assunta, we felt honored and marked the calendar for the coming Thursday.

On the day of the event Laura got out one of her best outfits and made sure it was freshly pressed. I dug around the closet for a pair of pants, not jeans, and later in town, at the Thursday morning market, used the occasion as an excuse to purchase a dress shirt costing all of five euros. We cut lunch a little short to be sure we were rested and ready. We elected to drive into town and had surprising difficultly locating an available parking space anywhere near the chapel. Concerned about the time, I dropped Laura off at the corner and drove farther into town. After cruising about, I located a spot at the far end of a municipal lot. As I locked up the car, I noticed a number of friars scurrying toward the chapel along with a number of smartly dressed couples. It took a few minutes to cross the parking lot and then make my way up the hill to the chapel. As I approached the chapel, I found a dozen or so people standing outside. As I got closer I noticed that the chapel doors were opened wide to an absolutely packed, even overflowing, church. As I realized there was no way I could make my way inside, Laura worked her way out to me, exclaiming it was hard to breathe in there and impossible to see anything once the bishops and thirty some priests and friars had made their way down the aisle. Wondering if it was the nuns or the bishop who had so many friends, I turned and saw Eugenia, a pleasant young lady vacationing from Rome. To my delight, she had found me a source for practicing her English. We met a week or so earlier in the town barber shop, where she had accompanied her aged grandfather. She noticed my struggle to instruct the barber not to cut my hair too short over the spot where I was balding, and provided the necessary translation. She then helped me to explain that it really wasn't necessary to blast country music at high decibels from his CD player in honor of his first American customer. Coming from the New York metro area, I never developed a fondness for the genre and felt it important for the kind fellow to devote his full attention to the head of grey hair in front of him, while preserving my hearing. And now, meeting again in front of the church, I expressed my surprise at such a large crowd, especially considering that attendance at Sunday Mass was usually pretty sparse.

She shrugged, responding that today's crowd was to be expected. "The church usually fills up whenever they are serving food," she said.

JUST ENJOYING THE DAY TO DAY

August wound down and Laura and I delighted in a change of pace. Finally we had a quiet week, which we welcomed as a chance to slow down and to get ready for another artist and seven students, as well as some more friends from home.

We took advantage of the down time one Monday to take a ferry to Isola del Giglio. It is a beautiful island about an hour and a half from Porto Santo Stefano, and therefore just two and a half hours from Farnese. When it comes to island beauty, it would stack up against Capri or Nantucket any day. (It is the island that gained international attention in 2012 when a cruise ship disastrously crashed into it.) We met a couple from Kinnelon, New Jersey on the boat and enjoyed talking with them. They took a Vespa around the island, but Laura was a little cautious so we hiked about and then took a taxi to the mountaintop, which contained a fortress going back to ancient times when the island served to protect the harbor in Rome.

We found a lovely beach and enjoyed a swim in the cool refreshing Mediterranean Sea, then spent what might be considered an inordinate amount of time at a seaside restaurant, accompanied by the local fish chowder, which reflected the day's very bountiful catch.

Back in Farnese, we happily began what then started out as a typically charming day. Laura and I were walking into town for our morning cappuccino. Nothing was out of the ordinary. We passed the cluster of men sitting with their backs to the wall, which our young friends referred to as the "national pastime." And then we went by some clusters of women doing the same. Unlike the men, the women chatted with each other and sometimes gave us a "*buongiorno.*"

We passed the white Vespa that was parked at the side of the road most mornings. It always appeared to be in pristine condition. Immaculate. I fantasized that it was mine and I was roaring down the hill and into the center of the town, cruising under the arches just like a true Italian. So I suggested to Laura that maybe I could buy one. Her look told me to get real. Oh well.

I was thinking about the possibility of running into some friends at Rokkabar. Maybe even the two friars from Africa named Gratias and Deo Gratias. Yes, those are their real names. Thanks and Thank God. All of a sudden there was a squeal of brakes, and we looked up to see Amabile, our cook and now good friend, stop in the middle of the road to wave to us, as a cyclist slammed on his brakes and barely avoided flipping heels over head onto the roof of her little blue Fiat. I had visions of the poor guy being scraped off the roof of the car like a stick of gum.

Amabile gave him a look of disgust before turning back to us to exclaim how that careless bicyclist nearly hit her car and without seeming to draw a breath, dove into a conversation with Laura.

Just a typical morning, until we got back to the *borgo* where Laura was accosted by La Signora, who had unexpectedly arrived complaining that the morning glory did not bloom, and what kind of a gardener was Laura anyway, and then began barking that a guest, Missy's boyfriend, had to be an absolute wild man. At this Laura struck back. Enough was enough. I had to enter the fray and explain that Missy's boyfriend had never set foot in Casa di Pietro, the scene of a broken chair. It was a continuation of the uncomfortable dialogue that La Signora had started about a month ago, and one which she would not let go. The stretcher on an inexpensive chair had been broken, and an angry Signora assumed that, since Missy, our son's young sister-in-law, stayed one night in the apartment, Casa di Pietro, she took to violently destroying the furniture. I patiently tried to explain that Missy was very much a lady, who would not take to destroying furniture, and that since she barely weighed a hundred pounds, she wouldn't be very good at it, if she happened to be so inclined.

Laura had suggested that Signora's friends from France, who had stayed in Pietro just before Missy, may have inadvertently caused the chair to split by sitting on it. After all, two of them were very large. What Laura said made a lot of sense, but in retrospect probably would have been more sensible left unsaid. La Signora had hit the roof. "How could anyone imply that about such honorable people?"

"Surely they were honorable but one being an opera singer, while lovely, was a substantial person. And they did live in that apartment for several days," I countered.

And it never ended. She could not let it go and kept bringing it up for over a month. We had insulted her friends, and somehow we were responsible for the broken chair. Eventually, I must have worn her down and convinced her that Missy, whom she had never met, could not have been the culprit, but then her paranoia got the best of her and determined that it must have been Missy's boyfriend. And so the mystery remained.

Soon La Signora herself would leave for Paris, and we could count on quietude until she returned to count the towels, sheets and kitchen utensils before we were scheduled to leave, for it was already October. But before leaving, she announced that someone had stolen a hibiscus plant. Probably it left in one of our guest's suitcases and has a new home in America.

TRYING TO MAKE IT LAST

The time with Dmitri and Karen had been terrific. They are interesting and kind, and he is a very special person. Google Dmitri Wright and you'll find a ton of photos and a video that say more about his life than I ever can. Dmitri and Karen felt that his programs were gaining momentum because the students returned home ecstatic about their time in Farnese. I did some preliminary numbers, and it appeared that we made a little money, while having the summer of a lifetime. It was unfortunate that the situation with La Signora prohibited us from continuing to develop the *borgo*. So we began to look into a site for the next year, having concluded that as great as the *borgo* was, La Signora was just more than any of us wanted to contend with.

We had a new friend, Shawn, over for dinner. Apart from us, Shawn was the only American in town. He moved from San Francisco to Rome, then discovered Farnese and fell for it so hard he became a walking welcome wagon. He had recently closed on some land and was busy preparing to plant fruit trees to go with the olive grove. He made arrangements for us to look at a property on a Friday. We became excited about the thought of continuing life in Farnese, but without having to deal with La Signora. We knew the property had spectacular views and a swimming pool, but suspected it would be on the small side when it came to bedrooms and baths. There was also the convent with awesome gardens and views in town, and a B&B we planned to look at later in the week.

THE HUNTING SEASON APPROACHES

There were signs of fall in the air. The days continued to be delightful. What makes the Italian sun different? But the nights were now cooler, as were the earlier mornings. Another indicator of the changing seasons were the tables in the *piazza* outside the Rokkabar. No longer were they spread across the *piazza* from corner to corner. Only a few dozen remained, and before long there would only be six or so left, just outside the door. Just as they were when we first arrived in May.

Some mornings we saw fog lingering over the olive grove, shrouding the fields and masking the hillsides. It was a whole new kind of beautiful. As fall approached, interest in the town turned to the hunting season. Hunting is ingrained in the Farnese tradition. The morning's first light was often accompanied by the sound of gunshots. Liam expressed concern about the laws that govern—or didn't govern—the hunt. It seems that hunters have the right to pursue their prey on anyone's property, as long as they do not go closer than eighteen feet from the house. A couple of hunters crossed into Liam's olive groves, quickly attracting the attention of Spike, Liam's dog. Actually, Spike is only half dog. The other half is wolf, and Spike is ever loyal to his duty to protect the pack, who in this case happen to be Liam and family. Apparently, ever dutiful Spike attacked the hunters and inflicted some significant damage to their prize hunting dog. I heard the story of how Spike once chased down a car and sent it to the local body shop, so I shudder at the thought of what he may have done to the hunting dog. Last we heard there was talk of a lawsuit.

But the big hunt, the premier league if you will, is the hunt for *cinghiali*. They are the wild boars that roam in abundance in the 50,000 acre Lamone Preserve that surrounds the town of Farnese. This is serious stuff. The *cinghiali* must be hunted, for they are multiplying rapidly and are known to wreak havoc upon crops. And while largely nocturnal, the *cinghiale*, with its sharp tusks, can be a real danger to humans who happen upon their habitat. But there is a happy side, for once hunted down, the meat of the *cinghiale* makes for some grand dining. It is lean, flavorful and not overly gamey. Two thirds of Farnese's three restaurants take enormous pride in featuring the meat from these enormous creatures in various dishes. Giancarlo, who owns and serves as chef at Il Giardinetto, showed us, with immense pride, a photo of his team standing beside last year's kill of eighteen of the grand beasts. But this year he would not participate in the hunt due to a problem of immense proportions. The preserve is divided into sections, and each hunting team must only use their assigned section. Shawn, the American, was not able to obtain a hunting license the previous season, so he accompanied Giancarlo's team as a videographer. He loves his new life in this quaint town so much that he was anxious to share his happiness with the world, publishing his video of the hunt on YouTube. It attracted the attention of one of the forest rangers, who in his vigilance determined that Giancarlo and his dogs were hunting where or when they were not supposed to be.

As a result, he arrested both Giancarlo and the dogs. Giancarlo's license was suspended, and both he and the dogs were fined, which created problems for both the courts and Giancarlo. The courts could not determine how the dogs would ever pay their fines, and Giancarlo could not see the justice in fining a pizza parlor owner 3,000 euros based on a video. Particularly when he believed he had confined his hunting to the designated sector at the proper time. He was a true sportsman and although an Italian, he took the law to heart. YouTube just did not show it as it really occurred. Giancarlo had appealed and hoped that the charges would be dropped. The court did drop the charges against the dogs after determining that dogs were incapable of paying fines. But while the appeal was underway, he could not join the hunt. All he could do was accompany the team and maybe flush some *cinghiali* out of the brush, perhaps for Shawn to nab, who did now have his license.

HOLY POTATOES!

Be it the fine wines, the fruits and vegetables, or the world's best olive oil, the key to the richness of flavor in the region's goods lies in its rich volcanic soil. One pleasant surprise were the Italian potatoes. Having grown up in an Irish American household, I had been brainwashed concerning the "superiority" of the Irish potato. Remember the joke about a seven course Irish meal: a six pack and a potato, or remember how tough it was in the old days, when I had to walk five miles to school in the snow, carrying a hot potato to keep my hands warm, which I would later eat for my lunch.

Growing up, Dad would not allow Mom to serve pasta or rice. Potatoes were pretty much our only source of starch, and they never missed a meal. So when the former Marialaura Ferrini became known as Mrs. Terrence Coen and began introducing me to pasta and then Arborio rice, any love I had for the spud soon became a thing of the past. And then thanks to the rich volcanic soil in Farnese, all of that changed. Far and away, the world's best potatoes hail from Farnese and the upper Tuscia region of Italy, and cooks like Amabile, the local restaurant chefs, and now Laura, really know how to prepare them. They roast. They fry. They make gnocchi, a wonderful pasta made from potatoes and flour. And they enhance the already wonderful flavor with the oil from the Canino olive and *finocchio*, the wild fennel found by the roadside. Laura spent countless hours busily gathering the latter, sifting out the kernels and drying them in the sun.

There was a potato farm in the valley not far from the *borgo* and Laura developed an acquaintance with the owners. Rosa was an attractive woman who originally hails from Tuscany. She could often be seen perched atop her Fiat tractor cultivating the fields, while taking in the sun clad in a shoulder-less top. Her husband, Rosario, was a banker and a gentleman farmer by avocation, who planned his vacation in conjunction with the harvest. What fascinated us about the harvest was that they had given up on the fully mechanized approach (too dusty) in favor of using a tiller to churn the earth and bring the product to the surface. At harvest time, early in the morning, Rosa and Rosario would be joined by a dozen or so seminarians from a Franciscan monastery. Together they completed the process of gathering the harvest in buckets, which were then loaded into containers and sent to the neighboring village of Grotte di Castro and the co-op. When their work was completed, the friars would gather in clusters under the shade of the trees that bordered the now empty fields and break out a few beers.

Happily, Rosa set aside a basket of the large golden nuggets for us. She added some eggplants, tomatoes, zucchini and one very large cabbage to complement our holy spuds. For several nights they were a part of a scrumptious barbecue.

OIL OF THE CANINO OLIVE, LIQUID GOLD

Italy has so much to offer. Often in the haste to see as much as they can in the short period that their vacation time or travel budget allows, American tourists rush from one glorious site to another. Their Italy may be several thousand miles long but only an inch deep. Because Laura and I had the blessing of time and were covering our expenses running the *borgo*, we were determined to dig deep, and to *live* Italy not merely see it. So for four and a half months, we did our best to put roots down in Farnese and the surrounding Tuscia region. That meant we did not travel very far. An exception was a day trip to Santo Savino, a small town nearly two hours into Tuscany. The purpose of the trip was to visit Ross, a friend of a friend. Ross was an investor in the business I still had a slight affiliation with, who had left his native Ireland some years ago to marry the love of his life, who happened to be an Italian girl. To supplement his investment income, Ross played saxophone in a jazz quartet that did gigs up and down the Tuscan entertainment scene, and he also ran a small *agriturismo*. Our friend had suggested that the two of us get together and share notes on the *agriturismo* biz, so Laura and

I set out for San Savino one day, bearing gifts of Canino olive oil. I should note that if the visit were taking place back in the states, the gift of choice would have undoubtedly been a few bottles of wine, but here in Italy wines were not only incredibly abundant, but the Tuscan region also enjoyed a reputation for producing the finest wines in all of Italy. So we opted instead to bring the prized Canino olive oil.

I think it is hard to find an Italian who will not tell you that the local olive oil is the world's best. Indeed, they prize it so highly that Italians hoard it for themselves. In fact, so much of the Italian olive oil sold in the states and labeled "Product of Italy" is bottled in Italy but comprised of a blend of oils, from Italy and other countries, such as Spain, Greece, or Tunisia. It's good stuff, but not in the same league as the typical native Italian product, and the oil from the Canino olive stands head and shoulders above the yield from the typical Italian olive crop, in our estimation. Credit goes to the rich volcanic soil. Unfortunately, few outside the Tuscia region have the privilege of enjoying this product. For, like the best of the local wines, most is traded at what outsiders would consider bargain prices, then consumed locally.

As we pulled into our hosts' magnificent property, the first thing to catch our eyes was the large olive grove sloping down from the house. "Coals to Newcastle," I muttered to Laura. We met, shook hands and I immediately began rambling on about not knowing that our host's *agriturismo* grew olives. What did I expect, bok choy?

By the time we sat down to a lunch, anticipating some delicious Milanese rice that our hostess had prepared using a recipe from her home city, I had regained composure and listened silently as our host extolled the fruits of his olive grove, proclaiming that no region on the entire peninsula nor its appendage islands could produce an olive oil equal in texture and flavor to that of the Tuscan region. Enough already. I threw down the gauntlet and called for a blind taste test. All we needed were two small bowls and a few small slices of bread. Fausto, a guest from Milan and a neutral observer, was asked to officiate. Only he would know which bowl contained which product. I felt a surge of anxiety as if the reputation of all of Tuscia rested on our palates.

We each dipped, tasted and smacked our lips. Unanimously, the oil in the bowl on the right was everyone's preference. We eagerly turned toward the smiling Fausto, who looked at our host, shrugged, and proclaimed the bowl on the right contained the oil pressed from the Canino olive. With a look of surprise coupled with disappointment our host raised a toast to the olive trees of Tuscia before we all dug into a sumptuous meal.

A few of our olive oil producing friends in Farnese were focused on broader market potential, and since Laura and I come from that broader market, it was inevitable that they would get us involved. The first was Domenico, who came to know some of the outside world when he drove the Grand Turismo, a sightseeing bus, around Europe before returning to Farnese to tend his olive grove and others', including La Signora's. During one of our frequent conversations, the chain-smoking, booming Domenico expounded on the potential of Canino olive oil in the American market. Because this was a serious business discussion, and recognizing our language disconnect, he was compelled to practically shout, somehow thinking that speaking louder would allow his pontifications to penetrate my apparently thick skull. And all the while smoking without pause. It is worth noting that Domenico had a rather unusual manner of chain-smoking. Each of his shirt pockets contained a pack of cigarettes and each pack contained a different brand. One seemed to contain plain unfiltered smokes, while the other contained a longer, thinner, filtered tobacco stick. Domenico, in between coughs, would alternately light and smoke a cigarette from one pack and then one from the other pack. There seemed to be a steady rhythm to it, and when a conversation would finally end, Domenico would leave a small balanced mound of two different shredded cigarette stubs in his wake.

Domenico explained that he would talk with a cousin, who knew the ropes when it came to exporting to the American market. It seemed that no matter how arcane an endeavor, everyone in Italy has a cousin whom they could contact to help get it done. But as the weeks went by, neither the cousin nor Domenico was able to come through. Then one morning in October, not long before our scheduled departure, Domenico called to say that an associate had a contact in New York and wondered if we might bring some olive oil samples with us upon our return. We said yes, just bring them over any time before five, when we were scheduled to go out with Amabile and Reno.

Before we knew it five o'clock came around. Amabile and Reno pulled in the drive and neither Domenico nor the olive oil samples had shown up. So off we drove into the hills north of Farnese. Reno wanted us to check out an abandoned villa in the Lamone that he thought we might be able to buy on the cheap and convert into our own *agriturismo.* As it turned out the structure was clearly beyond redemption, but the ride was pleasant and the sights delightful. Reno knew the fifty thousand acre Lamone as well as probably anyone, having lived all his life in Farnese and having developed a business providing firewood from fallen trees for many of the households heated by wood burning stoves. As we headed back toward town, he mentioned that a client lived down the road and would we mind if he stopped for a quick visit.

"Sure. No reason not to," we replied. We left one unpaved road and pulled into another, then drove a few hundred yards before Reno pulled off to the side of the road. I looked around but could not see any house. Then a very un-Italian looking chap carrying a clipboard, apparently taking inventory of his olive grove, materialized. Upon spying Reno, who had left the car by now, he smiled and headed in our direction. The two of them hugged like long-lost brothers. When we were all out of the car, our new acquaintance approached, stuck out a hand, and announced in English, "Hi, my name is Andy. Pleased to meet you."

I was taken by surprise. Hardly anyone in Farnese spoke English, and here we were, way out in the countryside, meeting a person who seemed to be living in humble circumstances, and not only did he greet me in my own tongue, but upon learning that we were from Connecticut responded, "Oh, I was in Westport on Tuesday."

Incredible. The world must indeed be smaller than I thought. He insisted that we tour his house and share a bottle of wine. The house was a rather basic structure tucked into the lower hillside, but with immense pride, Andy pointed out the cistern that served as the sole water supply, the gasoline operated generator that provided a bit of electricity to the two-room structure, and the wood stove, which thanks to Reno served as the source of heat.

Over the bottle of wine, Andy explained that his home was in Bolzano near the Austrian border, which explained his blond hair and fair skin, but his heart was in Farnese, where he and his wife and son made it a point to spend at least one long weekend a month. In Bolzano he served as a partner with KPMG, and it was as such that he happened to be in Westport, Connecticut, visiting a cousin while traveling to New York for a business meeting.

Andy's story grew more interesting as he described how he happened upon a store in Grand Central Station that sold nothing but olive oil. His thoughts immediately turned to Farnese and his grower friends, and what he was convinced had to be hands down the world's greatest olive oil. So dressed in a business suit and tie, he popped into the store, introduced himself to the manager and proclaimed he could provide the world's best olive oil, and to prove the point he would provide some samples, no cost or obligation.

"This is the way I see it," he told us. "Here in Farnese, the growers produce such a superior product, but selling it locally does not pay more than five or six euros a liter. However, in the New York store, smaller bottles sell for five times that amount." "Just think," he said, "what selling to this market could do for people here like Domenico, who tends his grove and harvests his crop every November/December."

Domenico? The same Domenico, who we know and who asked us to bring samples to the states? Yes, the very same Domenico. And small world, our new friend Andy, just by coincidence, happened to be Domenico's friend, who had visited Westport, Connecticut, and the olive oil store in Grand Central Station, and who had promised to send over samples of the world's best olive oil. And so we had a mission and when the time soon came to return home added several samples of Canino's fine olive oil to our effects.

THE GRAND FINALE

By October, visitors had stopped coming to Farnese. The summer had faded, and even at eight in the morning remnants of the night chill still hung in the air. The chill seemed to confirm our decision to say goodbye to the *borgo* and Farnese. I zipped up my sweater and opened the gates to the road, when I spotted an Irishman perched high atop his tractor, rumbling up the road with trailer in tow. His leather jacket seemed to underscore that our magical summer had come to an end. But it was not just the change in seasons that hastened our departure. Even in October, once the sun rose higher in the sky, it was enough to warm the soul. It was time to pull the plug on La Signora's ceaseless harping.

She had a way of forgetting what we had mutually agreed upon and that, by our final accounting, we had produced more income for her than she probably realized from the previous ten years combined. She had clearly gotten to us. She would leave from Farnese to Rome only to return in a day or two, demanding another meeting to once again review accounts or bellow about the broken chair. The meetings were for the most part repetitive with an occasional new wrinkle such as, "I don't see why I should pay a share of the common gas bill since I did not take many showers."

We were convinced that she had had every intention of pocketing the security deposit and advances we paid against utilities. She never was able to produce the utility bills, but we were able to confirm estimates through contacts Laura had made at the electric company.

Liam and I made fast work of stashing my bikes, the chairs, fans, and other items we had purchased to accommodate our summer guests in a trailer and in the Peugeot, then we headed off to stow them in his spacious *cantina*.

Laura and I had planned a going away lunch for our friends and helpers that afternoon, and Domenico had innocently passed word of it on to La Signora. We became concerned she would arrive and make another scene like the time when she invited herself to join us and a group of our guests and friends for a dinner at the lake and then reneged on her full share of the bill because she professed to not like one of the dishes. The day before, we determined that for everyone's sake and in particular our own peace of mind, we would pack up and be on our way. The lunch was quietly moved from the *borgo* to a restaurant. Subsequent "love letters" that hit Laura's inbox confirmed that a surprised and frustrated Signora arrived at an empty *borgo* at approximately the same time we sat down in the restaurant for our going away fiesta.

The lunch was a fitting wrap up. The men, with one exception, gathered at one end of the long table, Liam interpreting for me, while the ladies clustered at the other end along with Friar Deo Gratias, who no doubt stationed himself there to take in their conversation about Italians' favorite topic, food.

During lapses in the conversation I found myself reflecting again about how we had not merely visited Farnese. For nearly half a year, we had truly lived Farnese. We were not just tourists looking in from outside, but were truly engaged.

No doubt, after a few weeks in Connecticut, I would find myself wondering if Farnese ever did happen or was only a dream. Did it come into existence out of time and place only to disappear again? Out of time perhaps, but out of place only in contrast to the high intensity world I had come to see as my life.

In spite of the incendiary devices planted by La Signora, the road we traveled in Farnese took our lives to new and wonderful places. We experienced richness in both the magnificence and minutiae of daily life. Beauty in simplicity. Admiration and fascination with farmers who tended their lands just as their fathers and great-grandfathers had; restaurateurs whose menus contained the fabulous dishes they learned to cook from their mothers and grandmothers; husbands who lingered day in and day out over card games at one of the town's two bars; and housewives who simply lingered.

And it was a life so pleasing to the senses. The beauty around us stretched from the scarcely discovered beauty of Lake Bolsena, Europe's largest but most sparsely populated volcanic lake, to silver-hued olive orchards; from the vertically arrayed geometry of hillside vineyards to the medieval architecture; and from Etruscan ruins to the playboy ports along the Mediterranean Sea.

All this was a far cry from the hustle and bustle of our previous life among hedge fund managers, advertising gurus, soccer moms, and various others, intent on mastering the universe from suburban Connecticut. I can't say we looked different when we returned, maybe a bit tanner, but we had grown a lot.

VIEW MORE PHOTOS:
HTTPS://WWW.TERRENCECOEN.COM
/#FARNESE-GALLERY

EPILOGUE

Farnese did not disappear. The partnership with La Signora clearly did. We had demonstrated that with proper management, the *borgo* could house a successful B&B, and we turned a good profit for La Signora, while covering most of our own living expenses and the cost of bringing the family over for a truly unique and unrivaled vacation. But no joy existed in our relationship with La Signora. She spent part of the fall and winter attempting to recruit the art instructors to return to the *borgo*, working directly with her, and when that did not work she went after their students. In between she saw fit to drop us a nasty e-mail or two. But we managed to set aside that aspect of our Italian experience and determined that we wanted to make Farnese and the friends we had met there an ongoing part of our lives. We contacted Shawn and got the e-mail address and phone number of the small villa with the stunning views and the swimming pool, thinking that given the state of the economy they might not find it easy to sell and would consider accepting a longer term rental. Much to our delight they did. The villa slept eight comfortably, and we were able to make arrangements with two very nice in-town B&Bs to accommodate overflow guests. The villa had a 1,600 square foot terrace, with views of hillsides, valleys and distant mountains on three sides and a 680 square foot room below which made a suitable classroom or studio. The pool was large and refreshing and blended nicely into the hillside.

The friends are still here, and our friendships have deepened. La Signora is still here too, but we never ran into her on subsequent stays in Farnese. Upon reflection, we realized that she had added immeasurably to the dynamics of our Italian adventure, and for that we can be grateful. Our friendship with Amabile and Reno grew, and we learned from Amabile that La Signora renovated the *borgo* and art students continued to visit from the states. Amabile cooked for them. We were glad for her and for La Signora as well.

We never for a moment regret not having gone for a more conventional retirement.

ACKNOWLEDGEMENTS

Thanks to the friends on both sides of the Atlantic who encouraged and helped me to write this account.

Bob Dowling first suggested that I expand on the e-mails I wrote from Italy and put my experiences in a book and Tom Sand, who, like Bob, has a publishing background and supported the idea.

Ken Ottmar, who teaches creative writing, gave me the impetus to pick up the project after I had pretty much abandoned it and Bonnie Brien, who provided so much editorial help.

Finally two family members helped complete the project. Laura reviewed the manuscript to be sure the Italian words were correct in spelling and usage and Daniela Coen Clark, who served as production editor.

Laura also added the recipes that follow. She did so with the thought of helping our readers better share our Italian experience. Try them.

APPENDIX

Le Ricette Italiane

Marialaura Ferrini

-Antipasti and Contorni-

STUFFED ZUCCHINE FLOWERS

3 tbs olive oil
36 unopened zucchini flowers
5 oz canned flat anchovies in olive oil, drained
½ cup dry bread crumbs
pinch of pepper

Preheat oven to 350. Brush a 20x12 pan with half the olive oil.

With your thumb and forefinger nails, cut the stalk at its connection point to the flower, and gently pull to separate it from the rest of the flower. This way, you will remove the stalk and pistil in one.

In a small bowl combine the anchovies, the bread crumbs and a touch of pepper until well blended. Carefully insert a little of the mixture through the hole where you removed the stalk and pistil. Arrange the flowers in one layer in the baking dish and sprinkle with remaining olive oil. Cover with foil and bake about 15 minutes till sizzling hot. Serve while hot.

Stuffing with Sausage
8 oz of sweet sausage, skin it and crumble it in a mixing bowl. Add 1 egg, ½ cup Parmesan and 1 chopped clove of garlic. Follow the above directions.

Another Option
My mother used to insert anchovies and a bit of mozzarella. Then she would prepare a paste with 1 cup water, 1 cup of flour. This is for approximately 2 dozen flowers. I never make that many so I accordingly reduce the water/flour mixture. Mix well then dip each flower in the flour paste and deep fry them until golden. Remove them with a slotted spoon to an absorbent paper towel. Serve hot.

BRUSCHETTA

(The "sch" in Italian is pronounced *SK*)

1 loaf of Italian bread
2 large cloves of garlic, peeled

Bake thick slices of bread in the oven (preheated at 350) till crisp and golden. Then rub them with sliced garlic cloves, sprinkle olive oil while warm. Sprinkle with salt if you like.

If desired, rub a ripe tomato cut in half then sprinkle with olive oil and salt.

You can make your own toppings with chopped tomatoes flavored with Italian herbs and olive oil, chopped mushrooms cooked in garlic and olive oil, purchased artichoke spread or olive tapenade, or fresh arugula sprinkled with olive oil and parmesan cheese.

MY MOTHER'S STRACCIATELLA SOUP

1 Container 32fl oz. of good natural chicken broth
3 fresh eggs
pinch of salt and pepper
¼ cup parmesan cheese

Bring the broth to boil and remove from heat. Beat the eggs in a medium size bowl. Slowly spoon and stir half of the hot broth into the beaten eggs. Put all back in the soup pot with the remaining broth. My Aunt Anna added a few tablespoons of semolina at this point, but my mother begged to differ. Bring to a boil. Pour in individual soup bowl and sprinkle parmesan cheese on top.

SUPPLI AL TELEFONO (ARANCINI)

3 cups cooked risotto (usually left over from a previous meal, so the rice is well flavored)
6 tbs breadcrumbs
12 2-inch thick slices of mozzarella cheese
6 tablespoons olive oil (approximate)
2 eggs

Take less than a tablespoon of the rice in your hand and flatten it. Lay a slice of cheese on top, then put the same amount of rice over it. Roll into a ball, then roll in the beaten egg and roll the ball into the breadcrumbs. Repeat until the ingredients are used up (should make about 12 balls). Chill for 30 min. (You can prepare them ahead and refrigerate even overnight).

Heat oil and fry gently, a few at a time, so that they become golden brown. Then remove them from the pan and place on a plate with paper towel. The cheese inside should be just melted, so that it stretches when cut. Best served hot, but also very good at room temperature or even cold.

By the way, it's called "al telefono" because it resembles telephone wire when it stretches.

-Primi Piatti-

SIMPLE TOMATO SAUCE

1/4 cup extra virgin olive oil
2 large garlic cloves
1 large can of plum tomatoes chopped
salt to taste
1 ½ tbs chopped fresh basil
freshly ground pepper to taste

Warm the olive oil and garlic in a pan over medium-low heat, until the garlic is golden. Add the tomatoes, salt, and herbs. Simmer gently for 15 minutes. Remove the garlic, if desired. While sauce simmers, with a masher chop the tomatoes to roughly puree them. (if you don't like chunky tomatoes, puree in blender or food mill). Cook pasta and when al dente, drain and pour sauce on it. Sprinkle parmesan cheese on top. Mix and serve.

SPAGHETTI ALLA PUTTANESCA

1 large can plum tomatoes
3 tbs extra-virgin olive oil
4 anchovy fillets
¼ cup sliced black olives
2 tbs butter
2 garlic cloves
1 tbs capers
1 tbs chopped parsley
1 small can plum tomatoes

Combine olive oil and butter with sliced garlic and minced anchovies, sauté gently until the garlic softens. Add the olives and the capers, the tomatoes previously passed through a sieve, and cook for approx. 15 minutes.
Cook spaghetti, drain and pour sauce over them. Sprinkle with the minced parsley.

SPAGHETTI AGLIO E OLIO E PEPERONCINO

1 lb spaghetti
3 garlic cloves
hot pepper
1/2 cup olive oil
1 tbs minced parsley

Cook spaghetti. Just before draining them, heat oil with garlic and
a piece of chopped hot pepper till the garlic is golden (do not
overcook or burn garlic). Drain spaghetti when al dente and put it
in the pan where you cooked the sauce and let them cook together
for a minute or so. Sprinkle with parsley and serve.

SPAGHETTI CACIO E PEPE

1 lb spaghetti
1/2 cup romano cheese (Locatelli brand), freshly grated
2 tsp pepper freshly ground, mixed in the cheese

Cook spaghetti, drain when al dente, reserve a bit of the cooking water. Put spaghetti in warm bowl. Poor cheese and pepper on spaghetti. Mix, and add a little of the saved water so that the spaghetti are not too dry.

PENNE ALL'ARRABBIATA

1 lb penne
1 lb fresh plum tomatoes peeled and diced
Hot pepper – be generous, penne should be hot
3 cloves garlic
1/4 cup olive oil
salt to taste
1 tbs minced parsley

In the oil combine garlic and hot pepper, sauté till garlic softens, then add tomatoes. Cook over medium heat for the time it takes for the pasta to cook. Drain penne, pour sauce and sprinkle with minced parsley.

PESTO SAUCE

½ cup olive oil
¼ cup grated parmesan cheese
¼ cup grated romano cheese
2 cups fresh basil leaves 3 garlic cloves peeled
3 tbs pine nuts

Place all ingredients in a food processor. Chop and blend till
desired consistency (1 minute+-)

AMABILE'S ASPARAGUS LASAGNA

3 cups shredded scamorza (smoked mozzarella)
1 cup shredded mozzarella
1 ¼ cup grated parmesan cheese
Besciamella sauce
2 lb asparagus (hard bottom snapped off)
2 liters (quarts) water
2 packages of no-cook lasagna (fresh lasagna sheets available at
Whole Foods)

Cook asparagus in salted water, drain asparagus (reserve some
water) and put it through a food processor. The asparagus should
be creamy and not running. If too thick, add some of the reserved
water.

Add the besciamella and 1/4 of the parmesan cheese and process
until asparagus and besciamella and cheese are mixed.

Cover the bottom of a baking pan with asparagus/besciamella
cream and cover it with the pasta. Cover first layer with scamorza,
mozzarella and parmesan and then alternate with pasta and creamy
mixture. End with creamy mixture.

Cover it tightly with foil. Put in preheated oven at 400 and cook for
35-40 min.

BESCIAMELLA

2 ¼ cup milk
4 tbs unsalted butter
4 tbs flour
¼ tsp salt
¼ cup grated parmesan cheese
a pinch of grated nutmeg (optional)

Heat the milk just below boiling point, keep warm. Melt the butter in a heavy based saucepan. Working over low heat, add the flour and stir with a wooden spoon to avoid lumps. Let the flour and butter paste and heat through for about 2 minutes. Do not let the paste brown. Add the hot milk a bit at a time, stirring constantly. Continue to add milk until the milk is used up. Simmer the sauce for 15 minutes, always stirring. Add salt and if desired, 1/4 cup parmesan cheese, and nutmeg.

GNOCCHI

1 ½ lbs potatoes (I use red skin ones)
approximately 1 cup flour
(I usually do 2 medium potatoes per person and ¼ cup of flour for
each person)

Bake the potatoes in oven until fork goes through easily. Peel when
cooled and put them through a ricer. Mix the potatoes with the cup
of flour and knead till you form a tender dough that does not stick
to your hands. Add flour as needed while you knead the dough but
remember too much flour will make your gnocchi too heavy. Cut
the dough in a few parts and roll each piece into a rope. Cut the
rope in more or less ¼-inch pieces and roll each piece off a fork to
create indentation/traditional gnocchi shape. Cover the tray with a
towel and transfer gnocchi to the tray in a single layer. Sprinkle
with semolina flour to keep them from sticking to each other. You
can refrigerate gnocchi up to three hours.

PASTA ALL'AMATRICIANA

This is the official recipe of the Comune di Amatrice, shared with me by Paolo Pagliarini with the extra instructions "This recipe is very simple, but follow it with precision for best results."

1 lb spaghetti
3-4 oz guanciale
2-3 oz pecorino
12 oz San Marzano tomatoes
1 tbs extra virgin olive oil
¼ cup dry white wine
salt and pepper to taste
1 whole peperoncino (hot red pepper)

Cube the guanciale and put it in a pan with the olive oil and hot pepper (whole). Roast on heat for a minute or two, incorporating the white wine. Avoid burning the guanciale or the hot pepper. Remove the guanciale from the pan and let it dry on a paper towel; set it aside and let it cool.

Add the tomato to the pan the guanciale was in and cook for a few minutes, adjusting salt to taste. Remove and discard the hot pepper. Add the guanciale to the sauce and cook it a bit longer, letting it thicken. Once the pasta is cooked al dente, put it in a bowl with the grated pecorino cheese. Mix the pasta and the cheese, then add the sauce.

AMABILE'S SAUSAGE AND ZUCCHINI SAUCE

4 medium grated zucchine
4 sausages with skin removed and crumbled (I usually use 2 sweet and 2 hot sausages)
2 garlic bulbs
½ onion sliced
salt and pepper to taste
romano cheese
2 tbs olive oil

In a saucepan sauté onions and garlic in the olive oil. Add sausages, well separated and chopped, and zucchini on medium heat. Stir often and when the zucchini are soft and sausage is cooked lower heat and cover frying pan. In the meantime you will bring water to a boil and cook pasta al dente (farfalle or fusilli).

Drain the pasta and place it in the saucepan and stir it for a couple of minutes so that it will absorb the sauce. You should have enough liquid in the pan but if the pasta seems too dry drizzle with olive oil and/or add a small amount of water. Sprinkle a generous amount of Romano cheese and serve.

ADRIANA'S PASTA WITH ROASTED PEPPER SAUCE

3-4 peppers green, red, orange, yellow
half onion sliced
3 garlic bulbs
1/3 cup olive oil
salt and pepper to taste
romano cheese

Roast the peppers, either on the burners or in the oven under the grill, till skin is burned so that they can be peeled. Let the peppers cool a bit then peel them. It is easy to do this under running water. Wash out the seeds and cut the tops off. Dice the peppers or cut them in small strips.

In a saucepan sauté the onions and garlic in the olive oil. When the onions are translucent add the peppers. Add salt and pepper to your taste. Cover and cook for about 10 minutes. In the meantime, bring water to boil and cook pasta (again small pasta such as penne, fusilli, farfalle. orecchiette etc.)

When al dente, drain it and put in the saucepan and stir in the pepper sauce. Sprinkle with the Romano cheese and serve immediately.

PASTA WATER

Since pasta is made of flour, it releases starch into the cooking water as it boils, creating a white, cloudy liquid that you want to keep. It will help emulsify and thicken your sauce.

Emulsification is the process of blending two liquids that would otherwise repel each other. Oil and water don't mix but when making pasta you want them to. You want the sauce to uniformly coat the pasta. The starch in your pasta water, is an emulsifying agent and also a thickener. So if you save some of your pasta water and then slowly mix a ladle-full of it into sauce, you're binding together the liquids and oils, creating something creamy and thick that also binds to the pasta.

If you cook alternative pastas made with lentils, black beans, brown rice or just about anything else, those are all wonderfully starchy as well, and that water also can be used as liquid gold. Pasta water works its magic in just about every kind of sauce. It can make an Alfredo sauce less greasy, and it can give a silky texture to a pesto and of course tomato.

Usually just a ladle of the emulsified water will do although for larger noodles like fettuccini or spaghetti, or when feeding a larger number, it may work best to pour the water into a sauce pan and then give the pasta a good swim.

RAVIOLI FILLING

1lb fresh spinach, washed with stem trimmed and steamed. Drain, cool and squeeze and chop
1 cup ricotta - drained
1 egg yolk beaten
1/8 grated nutmeg
1/4 tsp salt and pepper
1/2tbs Italian parsley
1/4 cup Parmesan cheese

Combine all the ingredients in a bowl, blending them with a wooden spoon. Cover and refrigerate.

Forming the ravioli

The process here is to lay down a strip of pasta, place little dabs of filling across the whole strip in 2-inch intervals, brush some egg whites in the spaces between filling, and then lay a second strip of pasta on top, pressing down to form a seal on all sides of every filling dab. This can be done with a ravioli mold, which makes it much easier, or simply on a flat surface. If using a ravioli form, you'll have perforations on your ravioli pieces and can carefully pull them apart. If not using a form, your next step will be to cut between the filling dabs, forming the ravioli pieces. A rolling wheel makes the cutting easy if you have one.

Cooking the ravioli

In a pot bring water to a boil with a tablespoon of salt. Drop the ravioli in and cook for 3-5 minutes once the water has returned to boil. Stir gently and taste to make sure they are ready. Use your favorite sauce and sprinkle them lightly with Parmesan cheese.

MAKING FRESH PASTA

2 cups flour
4 extra large eggs
Optional: salt and 2 tsp vegetable oil

On pastry board make a well in the center of the flour and break
the eggs into it. Using a fork draw the flour into the egg. When the
dough is too stiff for the fork, continue with your hands, forming it
into a soft ball. If the dough is still too hard, wet your hands to add
moisture to it. If it's too soft, dip your hands in flour. Repeat as
needed, and continue kneading for 10 minutes.

When the dough is even and elastic, cover it with an inverted bowl
and let it rest for 15 minutes. Then cut the dough into thirds and
start stretching it with a rolling pin or a pasta machine.

-Secondi-

CALAMARI WITH PEAS

1 lb of calamari (to be cleaned by you or the fish store keeper)
10 ozs frozen small peas
A small onion
¼ cup olive oil
A cup of vegetable broth or water
1 garlic clove
Salt and a pinch of hot pepper

Cover the peas with vegetable broth or water and the garlic clove and cook them till they are soft. Set aside but keep warm.

With scissors, cut the cleaned and rinsed calamari tubes into small rings about ½-inch thick. In a pot put the oil and the thinly sliced onion and the pinch of hot pepper flakes. Gently cook the onions until they are transparent, then add the rings and tentacles and salt to taste.

Cook the fish for a couple of minutes - if you cook the rings too long they will be tougher. The best way to tell if they are cooked is to taste one ring. Drain the peas, add them to the fish and cook one more minute while stirring. Taste for salt and pepper and serve.

CHICKEN CUTLETS

2 skinless and boneless chicken breasts
Flour to cover both sides of slices
Lemon juice
1/4 cup olive oil
Salt and pepper

Slice the chicken breast as thin as possible, and pound it thinner with a weight. Season them with salt and pepper and cover both sides with flour. Heat the oil and braise the chicken breasts on each side. Then squeeze the juice of one lemon over them - sizzle and serve with all the juices. Serves 4 people.

FILETTI DI SOGLIOLA (FILLETS OF SOLE)

4 fillets
3 tbs unsalted butter
2 tbs capers
1 lemon
salt and pepper
1 tbs each parsley and chopped onion or chives

Roll fillets in flour, heat 1 tablespoon butter and fry the fillets on both sides until golden brown and cooked through. Season and put on a warmed serving dish. Heat the remaining butter, add capers, chives or just onion and parsley, and the juice of half a lemon. Just heat it through and pour over the fillets.

COZZE ALLA ROMANA

6 dozen large fresh mussels
¼ cup olive oil
2 tbs butter, melted
3 garlic cloves
10 fresh parsley sprigs, leaves only
1 cup toasted bread crumbs
½ tsp black pepper
½ tsp crushed red pepper

Under running water, scrub and clean mussels well. Put mussels on the bottom of shallow pan. Pour olive oil over them. Chop the garlic and parsley together. Sprinkle the garlic, the parsley, the bread crumbs, black and red pepper over the mussels. Cover tightly with aluminum foil. Bake in a preheated oven at 325°F for 30 minutes. Serve with toasted garlic bread.

-Dolci-

PANNA COTTA

2 cups heavy cream minus 2 tablespoons to dissolve gelatin
1/4 cup sugar
1 1/2 teaspoon gelatin (1/2 packet)
4-8 tablespoons fruit puree for topping

Heat cream with sugar, simmering for 15 minutes. Sprinkle gelatin over two tbs of cream. Remove simmered cream from heat and add gelatin mixture, stirring to dissolve (to avoid lumps, push the gelatin-cream through a small strainer into the warm cream and stir). Pour 1/2 cup of this mixture into 4 lightly oiled metal molds and refrigerate 6 hrs. To serve, dip molds in hot water and run knife around the edge, unmold panna into individual serving dishes and top with sauce.

ZABAIONE

2 whole eggs
4 egg yolks
¼ cup granulated sugar
2 tablespoons Marsala wine

Zabaione should be made in a double boiler. Put all ingredients into the saucepan, cold, then put over medium heat, stirring constantly for about 15 minutes until the water boils. By this time the amount will have increased enormously. As soon as it thickens and is light and fluffy, pour into warmed glasses and serve. It can also be frozen in the glasses. If frozen, bring to room temperature and stir it before serving.

29195640R00151

Made in the USA
Middletown, DE
21 December 2018